The Patchwork
PATTERN BOOK

Reworked and adapted for American quilters by
CARTER HOUCK

E. P. DUTTON   NEW YORK

TRIP AROUND THE WORLD
or Grandmother's Dream
Crib or Lap Quilt

Alternate squares of light and dark patches radiating from a center square. Stitched in diagonal strips across the quilt.

You will need:
Dressweight cotton (see page 64)
1¼ yard of 45-inch wide cotton backing
Crib-size batting (48 inches × 60 inches)
White cotton thread
Finished size: 41 inches × 41 inches

Patterns of the patches used (actual size)
Add ¼-inch seam allowance

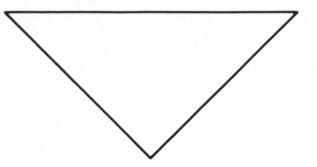

To make up

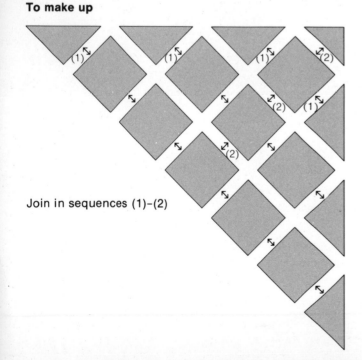

Join in sequences (1)–(2)

Continued on page 64

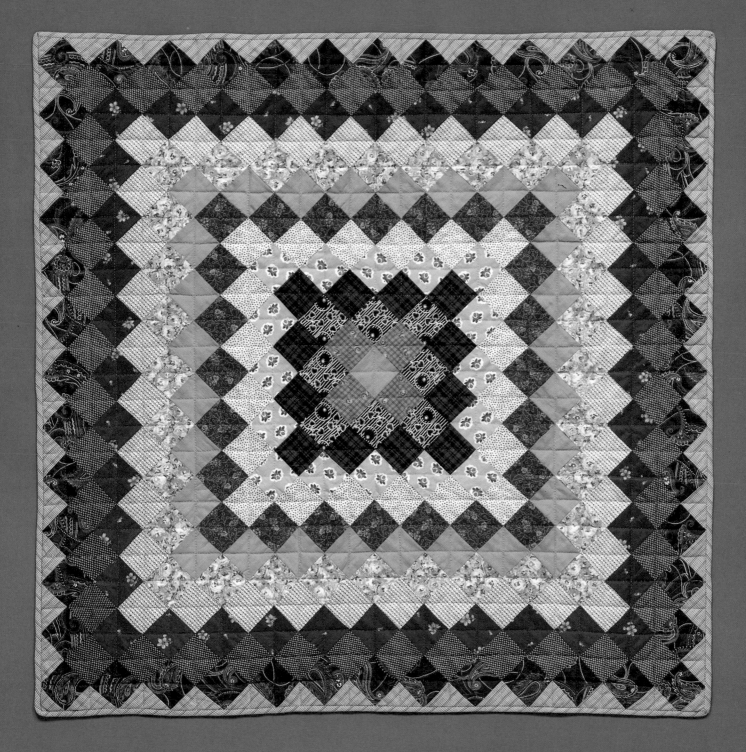

1

DOUBLE IRISH CHAIN
Crib or Lap Quilt

Alternate plain and pieced blocks. The plain blocks are quilted with a traditional design after the top is assembled (see page 67).

You will need:
2 yards of 45-inch wide olive green dressweight
   cotton (includes backing and binding)
1⅛ yard of 45-inch wide unbleached muslin
⅜ yard of 45-inch wide cotton print (a)
¼ yard of 45-inch wide cotton print (b)
Crib-size batting (48 inches × 60 inches)
Olive green cotton thread
Finished size: 39½ inches × 39½ inches

Patterns of the patches used (actual size)
Add ¼-inch seam allowance

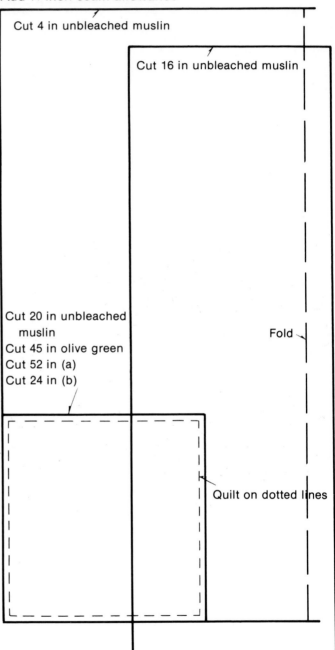

Cut 4 in unbleached muslin

Cut 16 in unbleached muslin

Cut 20 in unbleached muslin
Cut 45 in olive green
Cut 52 in (a)
Cut 24 in (b)

Fold

Quilt on dotted lines

To make up

Join in sequences (1)–(5)

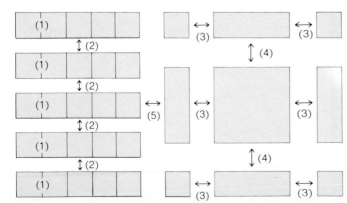

Continued on page 66

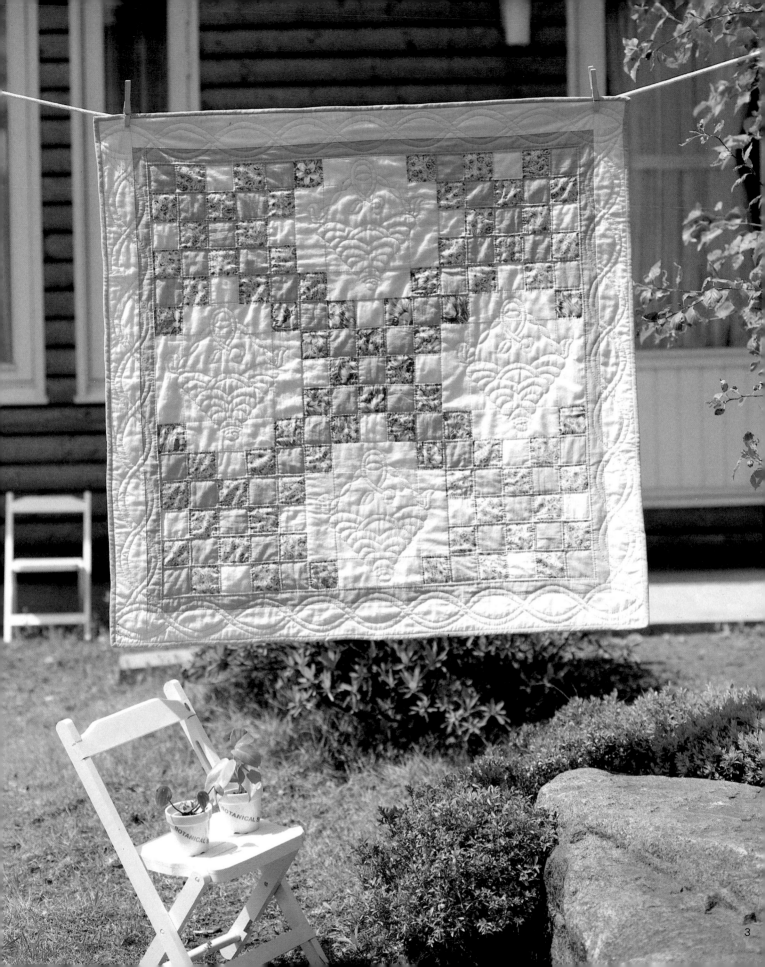

DOUBLE IRISH CHAIN
Youth Bed Quilt

(For a 73-inch × 87-inch single-bed quilt, add two rows of blocks to both length and width.)

You will need:
2 yards of 45-inch wide unbleached muslin
4⅛ yards of 45-inch wide navy blue dressweight cotton (includes borders and backing)
1 yard (total) of 45-inch wide print and solid dressweight cotton
Twin-size batting (65 inches × 97 inches)
Navy blue cotton thread
Finished size: 59 inches × 73 inches

Quilting design (actual size)

Patterns of the patches used (actual size)
Add ¼-inch seam allowance

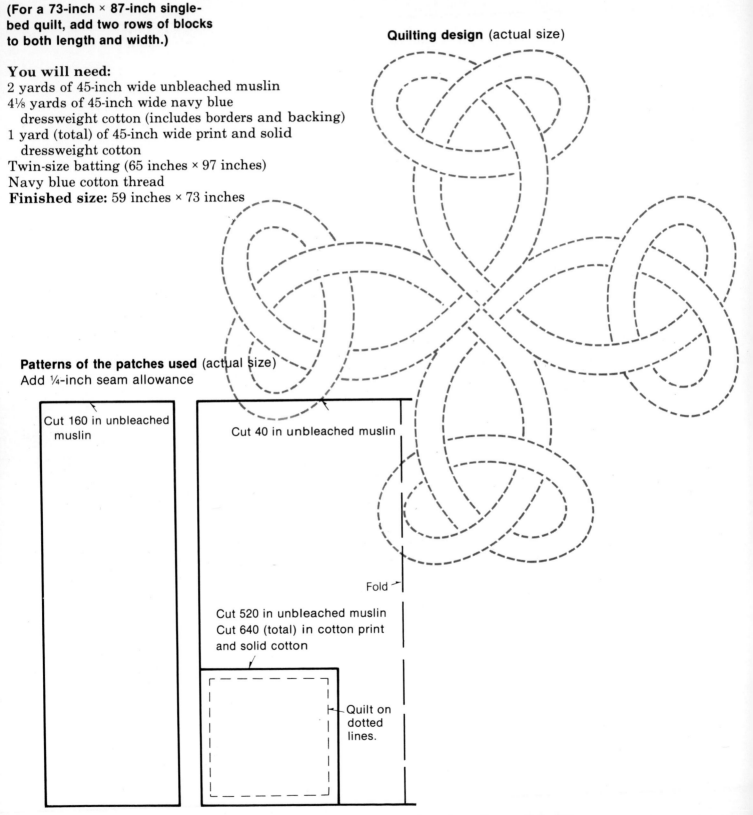

Cut 160 in unbleached muslin

Cut 40 in unbleached muslin

Fold

Cut 520 in unbleached muslin
Cut 640 (total) in cotton print and solid cotton

Quilt on dotted lines.

To make up see page 2

Continued on page 65

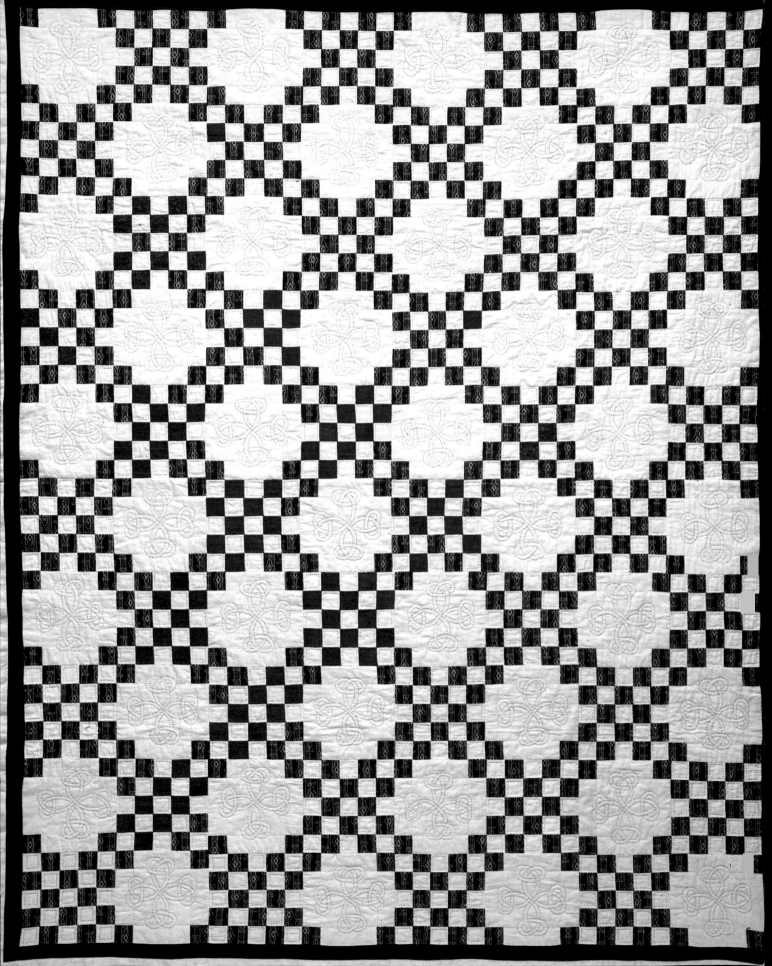

LOG CABIN
Lap Quilt or Throw

The narrow strips of fabric represent the overlapping logs of a log cabin. (For an 80-inch × 90-inch double-bed quilt, make 72 blocks)

You will need:
Dressweight cotton (see page 68)
2⅞ yards of 45-inch wide
  bright navy dressweight cotton
  (includes backing and binding)
Section cut from twin-size batting
  (65 inches × 97 inches)
Finished size: 50 inches × 50 inches

To make up
Join in sequence (1)–(16)

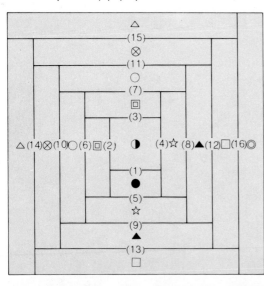

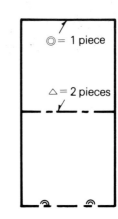

Continued on page 68

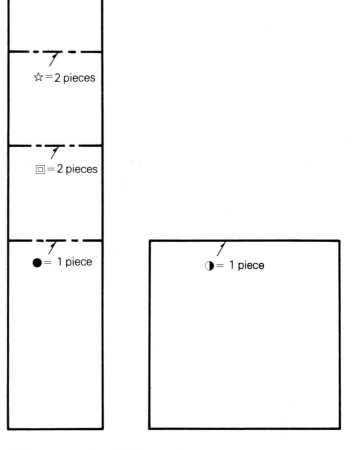

□ = 2 pieces

⊗ = 2 pieces

▲ = 2 pieces

○ = 2 pieces

☆ = 2 pieces

▣ = 2 pieces

● = 1 piece

Patterns of the patches used
(actual size)
Add ¼-inch seam allowance

◎ = 1 piece

△ = 2 pieces

Match pieces at
balance marks (☺).

◑ = 1 piece

This pattern gives the increasing
lengths for the fabric strips worked
around the center square (see left).

6

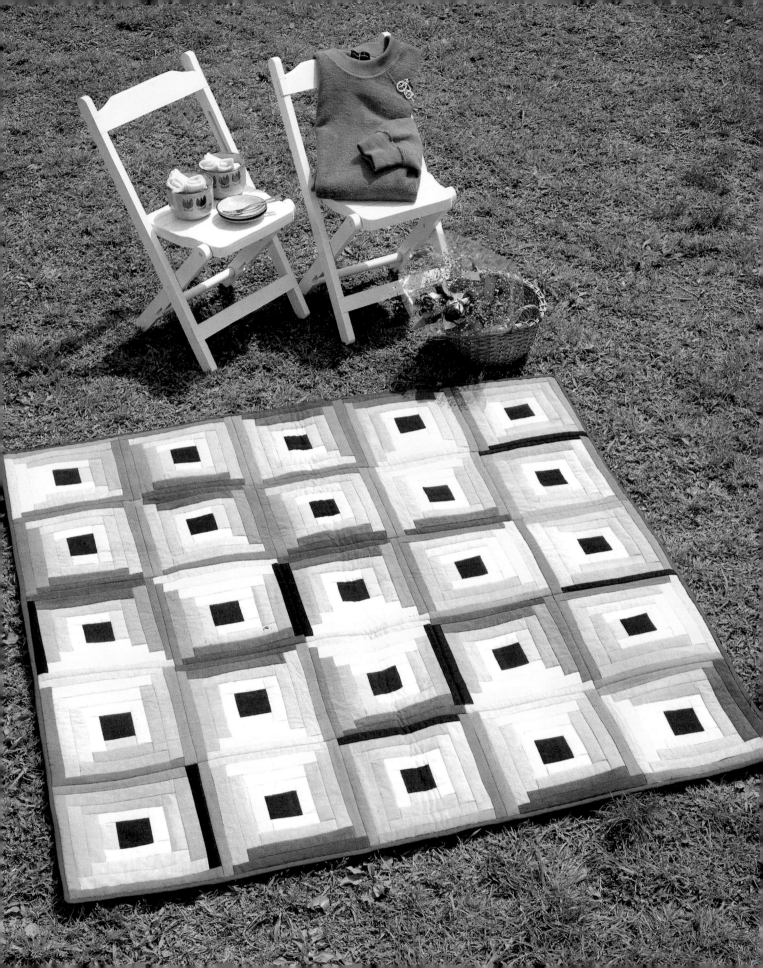

MOSAIC STAR
Crib Quilt

This design is composed of hexagons and pentagons and can best be made by using the paper-liner method (see page 101).

You will need:
1½ yards of 45-inch wide bright navy dressweight cotton
¼ yard of 45-inch wide yellow dressweight cotton
¾ yard of 45-inch wide blue polka dot print cotton
  (includes binding and some stars)
Scraps totaling 1½ yards of 45-inch wide print and solid
  dressweight cottons for 40 sets of 6 patches each
1⅞ yards of 45-inch wide dressweight cotton for backing
One-half of twin-size batting (65 inches × 97 inches)
Navy blue and yellow cotton thread
Finished size: 63 inches × 44 inches

To make up
Join in sequences (1)–(4)

Patterns of the patches used (actual size)
Add ¼-inch seam allowance

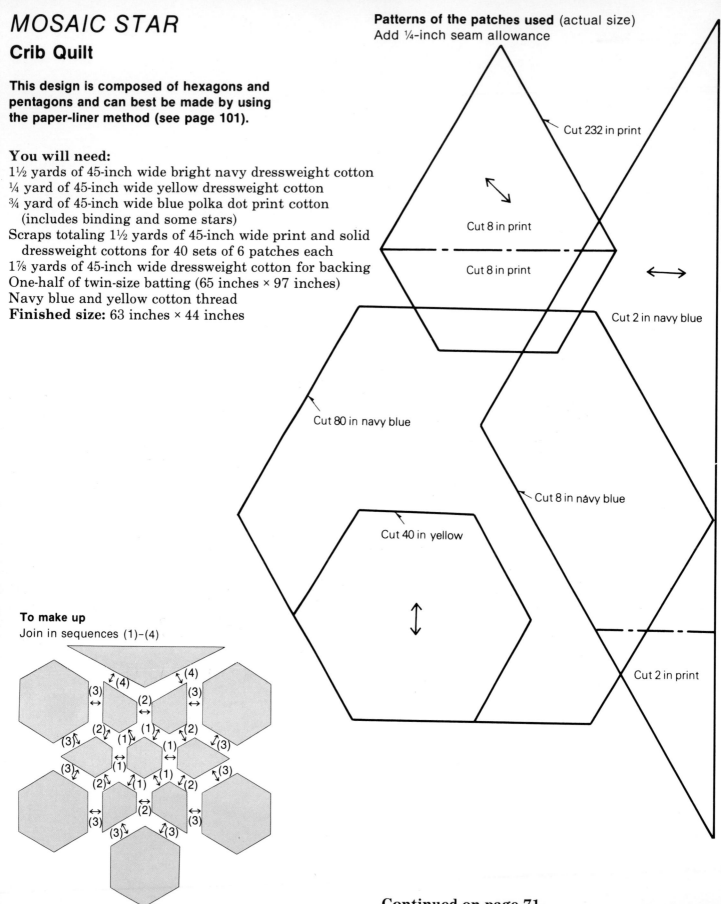

Cut 232 in print

Cut 8 in print

Cut 8 in print

Cut 2 in navy blue

Cut 80 in navy blue

Cut 8 in navy blue

Cut 40 in yellow

Cut 2 in print

Continued on page 71

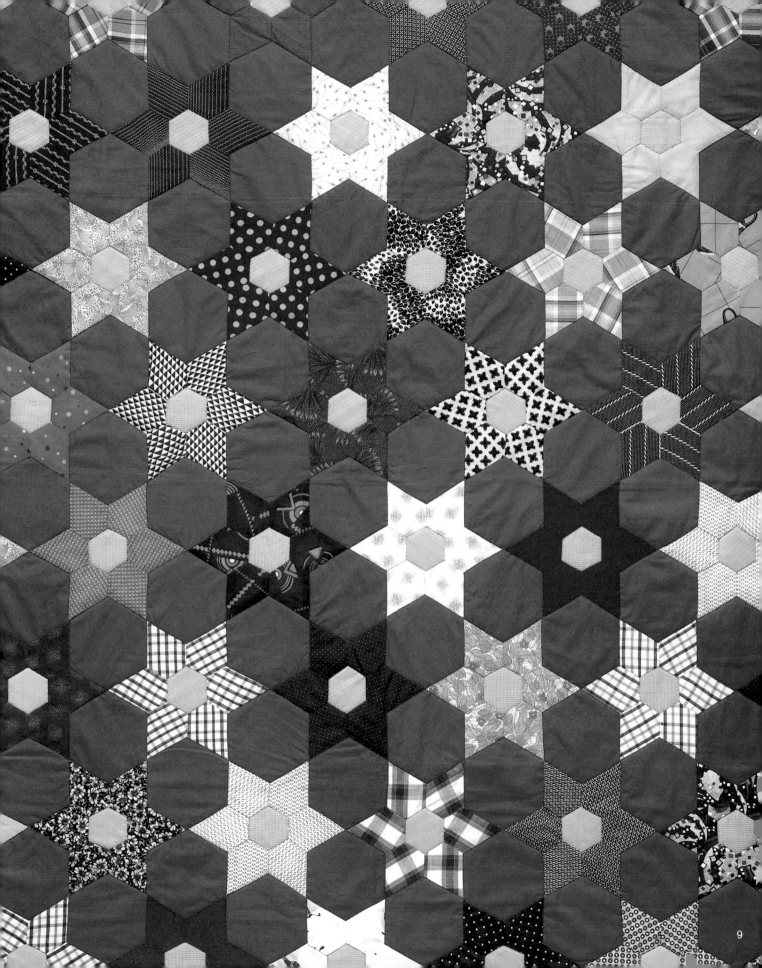

STAR OF BETHLEHEM
Tablecloth

Six diamonds at the center are extended to a large six-point star, another version of the eight-sided Star of Bethlehem or Lone Star.

You will need:
2½ yards of 45-inch wide royal blue dressweight cotton
½ yard of 45-inch wide red dressweight cotton
½ yard of 45-inch wide pale blue dressweight cotton
¼ yard of 45-inch wide blue-and-white polka dot print cotton
3½ yards of 45-inch wide white dressweight cotton (includes
   lining and diamonds)
Finished size: 60½ inches × 68 inches

Patterns of the patches used (actual size)
Add ¼-inch seam allowance

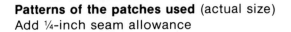

Cut 104 in red
Cut 98 in pale blue
Cut 54 in print
Cut 48 in white

To make up
Join in sequences (1)–(3)

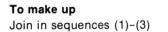

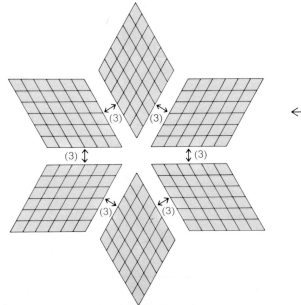

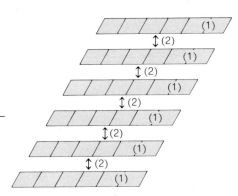

Continued on page 72

10

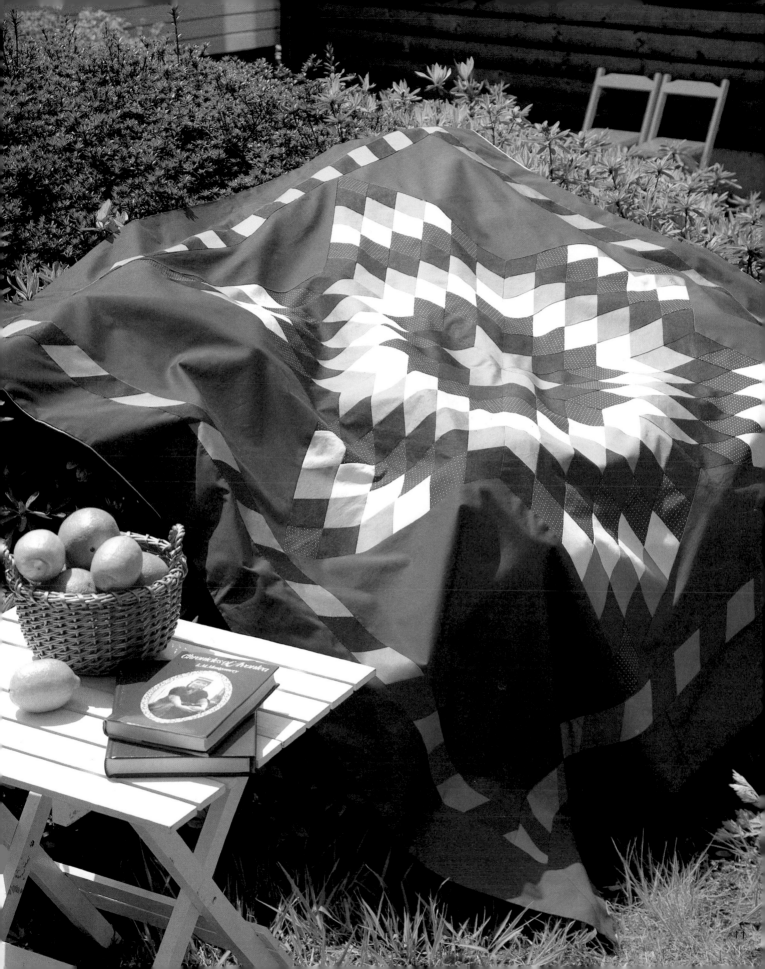

A THOUSAND PYRAMIDS
Bed Linen and Matching Picture

This design is composed of equilateral triangles in light and dark fabrics.

Patchwork Picture
You will need:
Scraps of pink, green, and print dressweight cottons
  (or ⅛ yard of each if purchased)
10-inch × 12-inch scrap cotton for backing
10-inch × 12-inch scrap of batting
Frame with inside measurements of 8 inches × 11¼ inches
  (or matting to that size)
White cotton thread
Finished size: 8 inches × 11¼ inches

Bed Linen (see note below)
For the patchwork border, you will need:
1 yard of 45-inch wide blue-and-white print cotton
½ yard of 45-inch wide light blue dressweight cotton
½ yard of 45-inch wide dark blue dressweight cotton
1½ yards of 45-inch wide cotton backing
Crib-size batting (48 inches × 60 inches) (optional)
White cotton thread
Finished size: 50 inches × 21½ inches

For the pillowcase, you will need:
½ yard of 45-inch wide blue-and-white print cotton
¾ yard of 45-inch wide light blue dressweight cotton
  (includes pillowcase back and some patches)
¼ yard of 45-inch wide dark blue dressweight
  cotton
⅝ yard of 45-inch wide cotton backing
Batting, scrap from border (optional)
White cotton thread
Finished size: 25 inches × 17½ inches
  (youth bed pillow)

Patterns of the patches used (actual size)
Add ¼-inch seam allowance.

Patchwork border
Pillowcase

Cut 4 in print for pillowcase
Cut 2 in both light and dark blue for pillowcase
Cut 6 in print for border
Cut 2 in both light and dark blue for border

Patchwork
Picture

Cut 10 in print

Cut 47 in print for border
Cut 24 in both light and dark blue for border

Patchwork border
Pillowcase

Cut 18 in print for pillowcase
Cut 9 in both light and dark blue for pillowcase

Patchwork
Picture

Cut 10 in print
Cut 9 in pink
Cut 6 in green

To make up
Join in sequences (1) and (2)

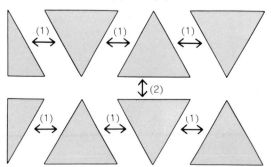

Note: Both pieces, as pictured, are backed but have no batting. For more effective quilting, use batting. The border is intended for use in making up a bed with a pretty blanket or blanket cover and no bedspread. It is long enough to tuck in on a youth bed or single-bed mattress and can be extended as much as desired by the addition of more patches at the ends. It can also be made to match the size of any sheet and sewn to the top edge of the sheet like a facing with no batting. It can then be machine topstitched in place along the seamlines.

Continued on page 69

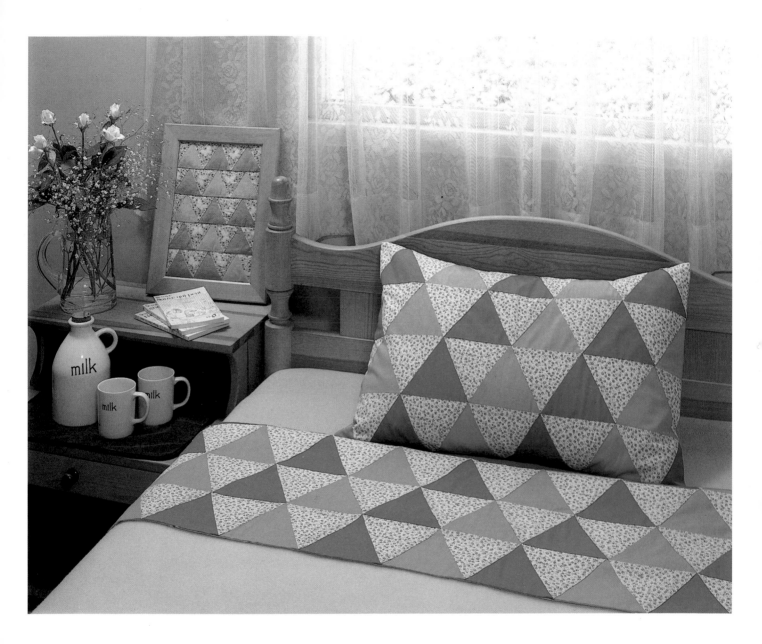

MOUNTAIN CHAIN
Placemats and Pincushions

A design made entirely of right-angle triangles.

Placemat
You will need:
(makes two mats in one color combination)
¼ yard of 45-inch wide print cotton (a)
¼ yard of 45-inch wide print cotton (b)
⅜ yard of dressweight cotton backing
⅜ yard of fleece type batting
3¼ yards of wide bias tape to match
White cotton thread
Finished size: 17 inches × 11½ inches

Pincushions A, B, and C
You will need:
Scraps of any combinations of print and
  solid dressweight cottons (or ⅛ yard of
  each if purchased)
Small amounts of synthetic filler or kapok
Finished size of each: 3½ inches square

Patterns of the patches used (actual size)
Add ¼-inch seam allowance.

Cut 3 in both light and dark

Placemat

Cut 12 in both light and dark

Cut 4 in both print and solid

Cut 9 in both print and solid

Pincushions A and B   Pincushion C

To make up
Join in sequences (1)–(3)

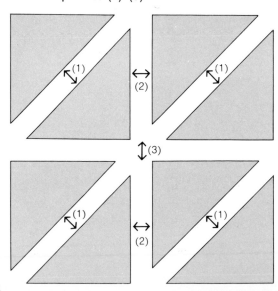

Continued on page 73

14

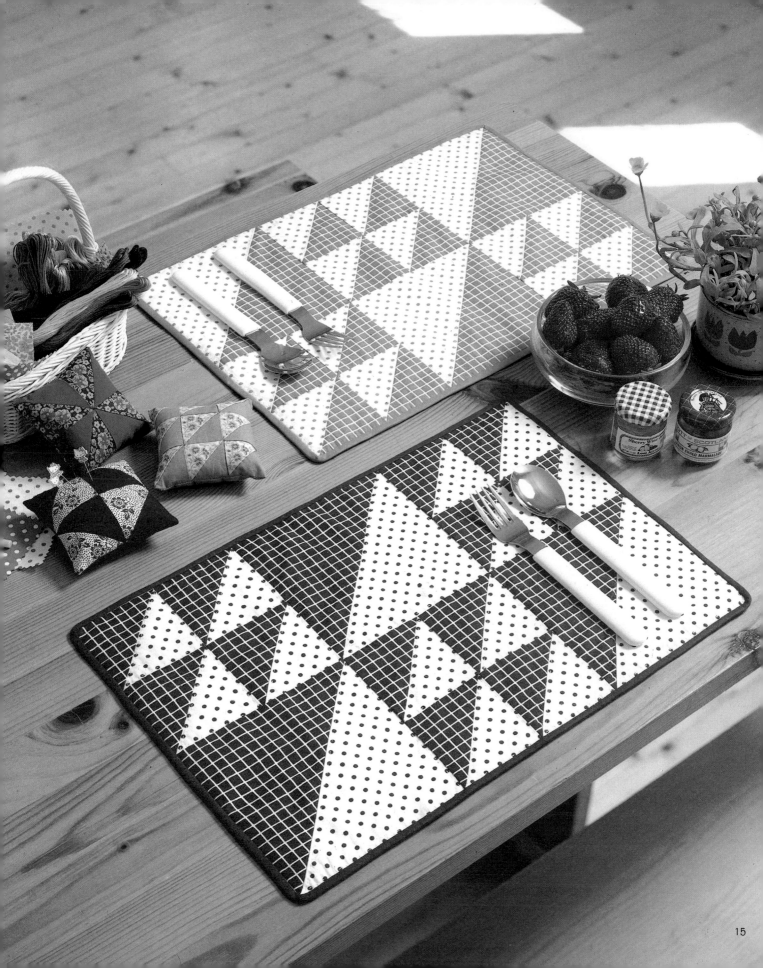

FRENCH BOUQUET
Tablecloth

Hexagons form the basis of this design, which is constructed in an unusual manner. Because of the large size of the pieces and the way in which they are pieced and attached to the lining, it is not necessary to use the paper-liner method.

You will need:
1½ yards of 45-inch wide brown dressweight cotton
½ yard each of three 45-inch wide print cottons (a), (b), and (c)
Brown cotton thread
Finished size: 40 inches × 46 inches

Patterns of the patches used (actual size)
Add ¼-inch seam allowance

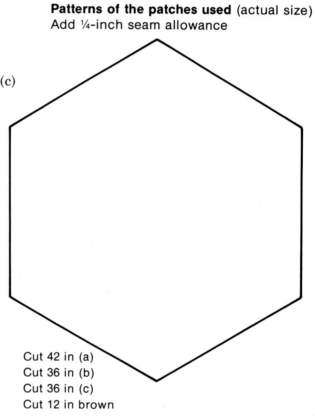

Cut 42 in (a)
Cut 36 in (b)
Cut 36 in (c)
Cut 12 in brown

Step 3: (detail)

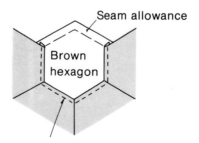

Seam allowance

Brown hexagon

Turn under the seam allowance around the 12 indentations along the edge of the assembled pieces and topstitch to the 12 brown hexagons, making the edge fall in even points.

To make up
Join in sequences (1)–(2)

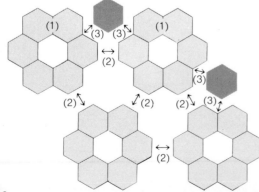

Continued on page 75

16

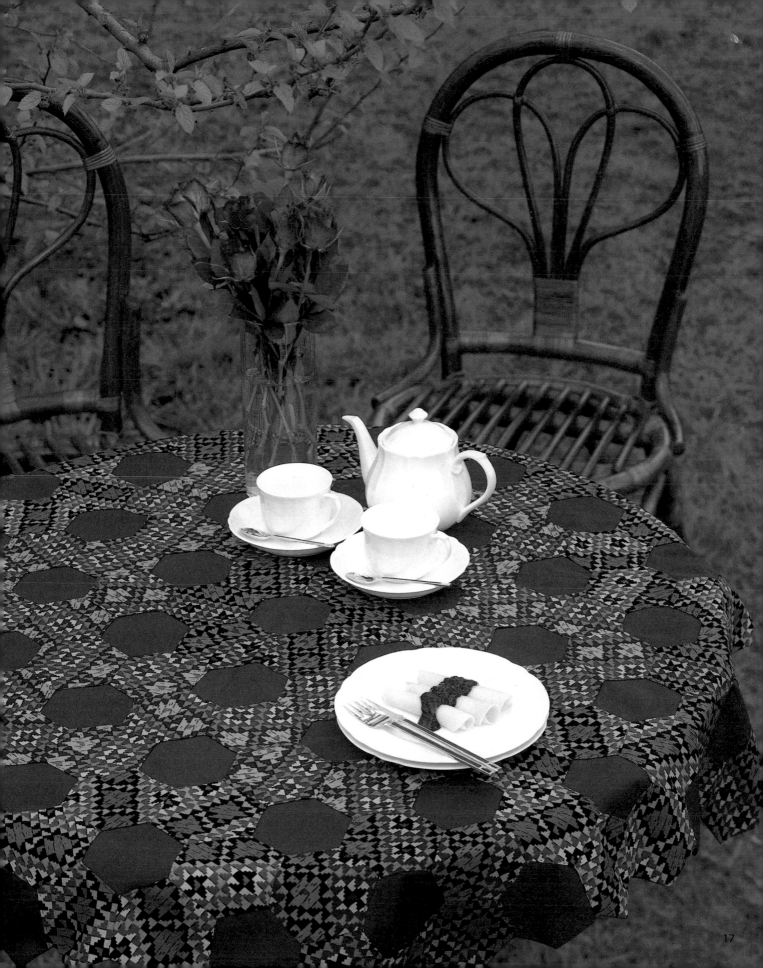

DRUNKARD'S PATH
Bed Linen and Tray Cloth

Curves and straight edges, and a variety of prints create varied and interesting effects.

Tray Cloth
You will need:
Scraps of four print cottons (a), (b), (c), and (d)
   (or ⅛ yard of each if purchased)
1½ yards of pink standard bias tape
12-inch × 15-inch scrap of cotton for backing
12-inch × 15-inch scrap of fleece type batting
White cotton thread
Finished size: 14¼ inches × 11½ inches

Bed Linen (see note below)
For the patchwork border, you will need:
½ yard of 45-inch wide print cottons for both (a) and (b)
¼ yard of 45-inch wide print cottons for both (c) and (d)
⅝ yard of 45-inch wide cotton backing
Crib-size batting (48 inches × 60 inches) (optional)
3¾ yards of 3½-inch wide white eyelet edging
Blue cotton thread
Finished size: 47 inches × 25 inches (includes eyelet)

For the pillowcase, you will need:
⅜ yard of 45-inch wide print cotton (a)
¾ yard of 45-inch wide print cotton (b)
   (includes pillowcase back)
¼ yard of 45-inch wide print cottons for both (c) and (d)
⅝ yard of 45-inch wide cotton backing
Batting, scrap from border (optional)
4½ yards of 3½-inch wide white eyelet edging (if used ruffled, as shown. 2¾ yards if used plain)
Blue cotton thread
1 inch narrow Velcro™
Finished size: 25 inches × 18¾ inches (youth bed size)
              31 inches × 24¾ inches (includes eyelet)

Patterns of the patches used (actual size)
Add ¼-inch seam allowance

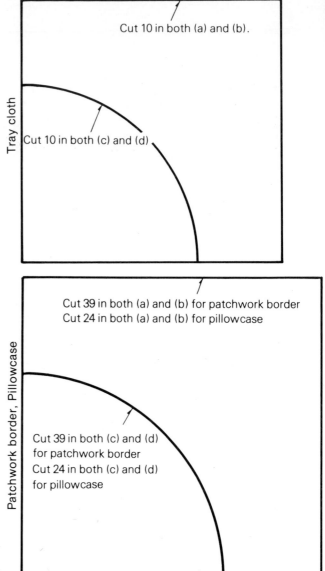

Tray cloth

Cut 10 in both (a) and (b).

Cut 10 in both (c) and (d).

Patchwork border, Pillowcase

Cut 39 in both (a) and (b) for patchwork border
Cut 24 in both (a) and (b) for pillowcase

Cut 39 in both (c) and (d) for patchwork border
Cut 24 in both (c) and (d) for pillowcase

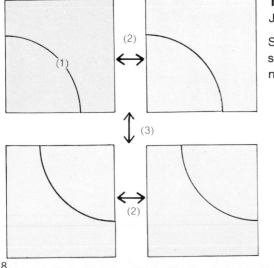

(1)
(2)
(3)

To make up
Join in sequences (1)–(3)

Seam the curves of the two pieces together, stretching and clipping the concave one as necessary.

Note:
Both pieces, as pictured, are backed but have no batting. For more effective quilting, use batting. The border is intended for making up a bed with a pretty blanket or blanket cover and no bedspread. It is long enough to go across a youth bed or single bed and can be extended as much as desired by the addition of more patches at the ends. The pillowcase can be enlarged in the same way.

Continued on page 73

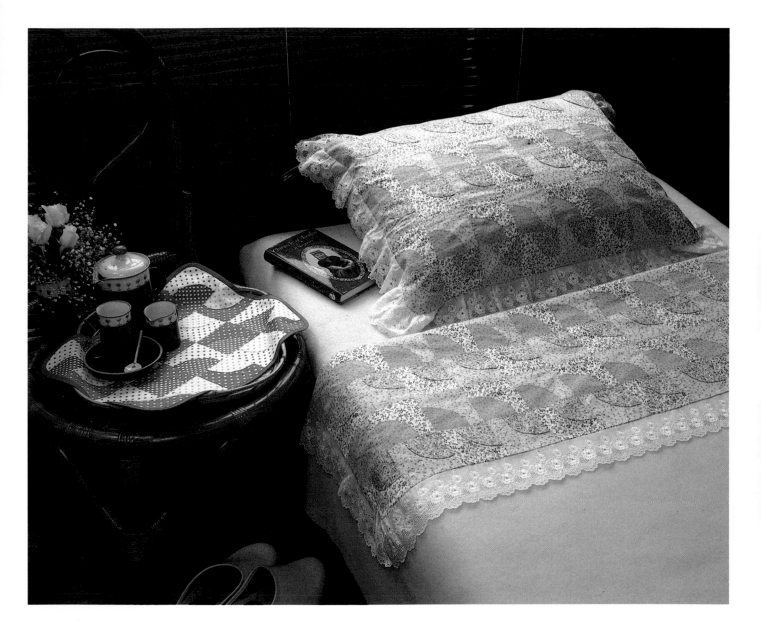

GRANDMOTHER'S FAN
Panel

Colorful fans in a variety of prints against a plain background make an attractive panel.

You will need:
1¼ yards of 45-inch wide beige dressweight cotton
1 yard of 45-inch wide print cotton (a)
   (includes binding and patches)
⅜ yard each of 45-inch wide print cotton (b) and (c)
½ yard each of 45-inch wide print cotton (d) and (e)
1½ yards of 45-inch wide cotton backing
1½ yards of fleece type batting (optional)
Finished size: 63 inches × 27 inches

SHOO FLY
Wall Hanging and Phone Set

The Shoo Fly design is a simple variation of the Nine-Patch.

Phone Set
For the phone cover, you will need:
½ yard of 45-inch wide brown dressweight cotton
   (includes backing and binding)
Scraps of four prints (a), (b), (c), and (d)
   (or ⅛ yard of each if purchased)
Finished size: 15¾ inches × 15¾ inches

For the mat you will need:
Remaining piece of brown dressweight cotton from
   cover (includes backing and binding)
12-inch square scrap of above cotton print (a)
   (or ⅜ yard if purchased)
12-inch square scrap of fleece type batting
Finished size: 12 inches × 12 inches

Wall Hanging with Pockets
You will need:
½ yard of 45-inch wide moss green dressweight cotton
Scraps of 2 prints (a) and (b)
   (or ⅛ yard of each if purchased)
¼ yard of 45-inch wide print cotton (c)
   (includes pocket binding and patches)
½ yard of 45-inch wide print cotton (d)
   (includes outer binding and patches)
½ yard of 45-inch wide cotton backing
½ yard of fleece type batting
1½ inches of narrow Velcro™
Finished size: 14 inches × 26 inches

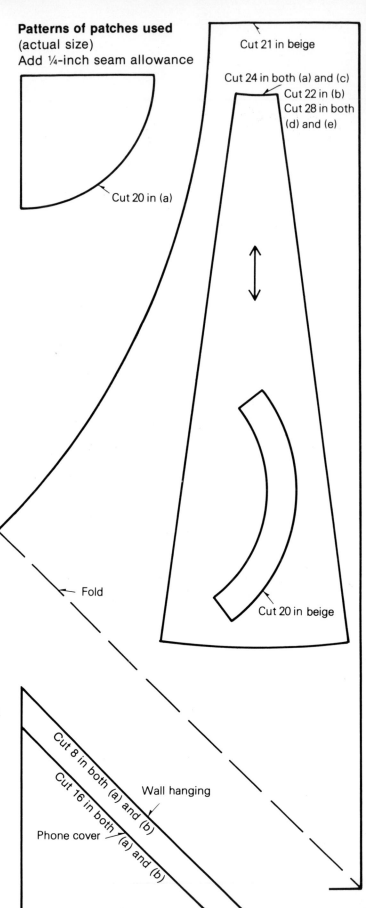

Patterns of patches used
(actual size)
Add ¼-inch seam allowance

Cut 21 in beige
Cut 24 in both (a) and (c)
Cut 22 in (b)
Cut 28 in both (d) and (e)
Cut 20 in (a)
Fold
Cut 20 in beige
Cut 8 in both (a) and (b)
Cut 16 in both (a) and (b)
Wall hanging
Phone cover

To make up   Join in sequences (1)–(4)

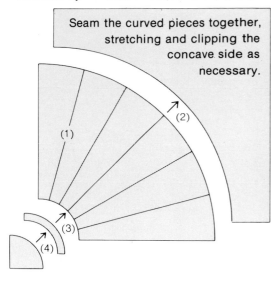

Seam the curved pieces together,
stretching and clipping the
concave side as
necessary.

Join in sequences (1)–(3)

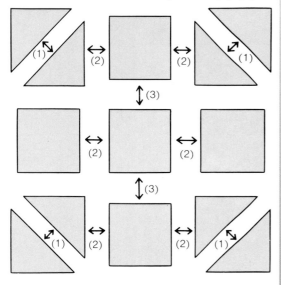

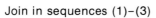

Wall hanging	Cut 8 in (c) Cut 2 in (d)
Phone cover	Cut 16 in (c) Cut 4 in (d)

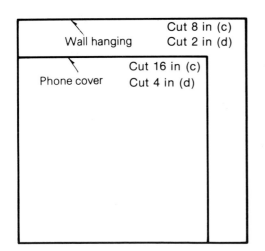

Continued on page 76

Continued on page 76

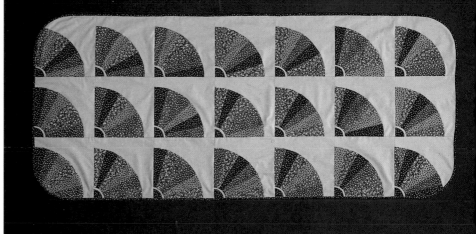

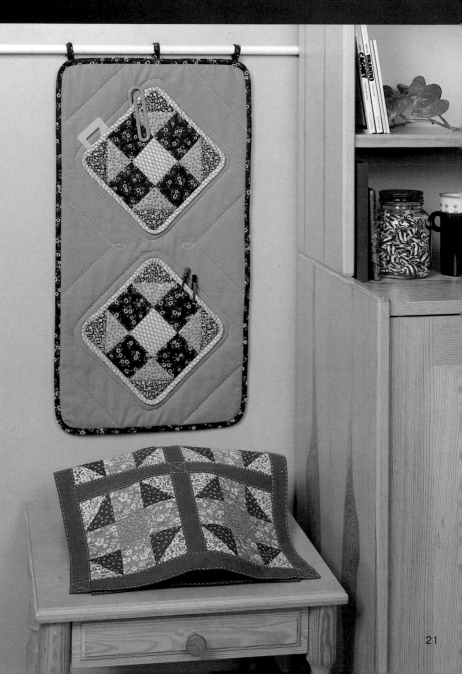

MAPLE LEAF
Table Mat and Potholders

Nine-Patch blocks, pieced from a combination of squares and right-angle triangles, make up the Maple Leaf design, a favorite in Canada.

Table Mat
You will need:
½ yard of 45-inch wide unbleached muslin
  (includes backing and some patches)
¼ yard of 450inch wide print cotton (a)
  (includes binding and some patches)
Scraps of print cotton (b) and (c)
  (or ⅛ yard of each if purchased)
½ yard of fleece type batting
Matching cotton thread
Finished size: 18½ inches × 18½ inches

Potholder:
You will need:
Scraps of print or solid cottons for (a) and (b)
  (⅛ yard of each if purchased)
Scraps of print or solid cotton for (c)
  (or ¼ yard if purchased)
  (includes backing and patch)
Scraps or ¼ yard of fleece type batting (use double)
¾ yard of wide bias tape for each potholder
Matching cotton thread
Finished size: 7 inches × 7 inches

Patterns of the patches used (actual size)
Add ¼-inch seam allowance

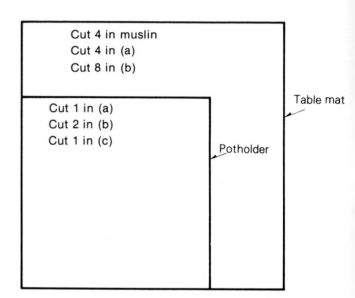

Cut 4 in muslin
Cut 4 in (a)
Cut 8 in (b)

Cut 1 in (a)
Cut 2 in (b)
Cut 1 in (c)

Table mat

Potholder

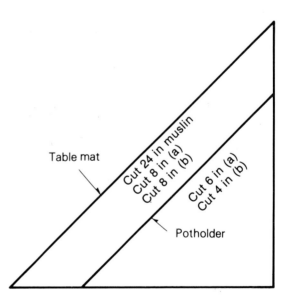

Table mat

Cut 24 in muslin
Cut 8 in (a)
Cut 8 in (b)

Cut 6 in (a)
Cut 4 in (b)

Potholder

To make up
Join in sequences (1)–(3)

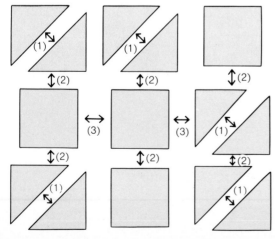

Continued on page 77

22

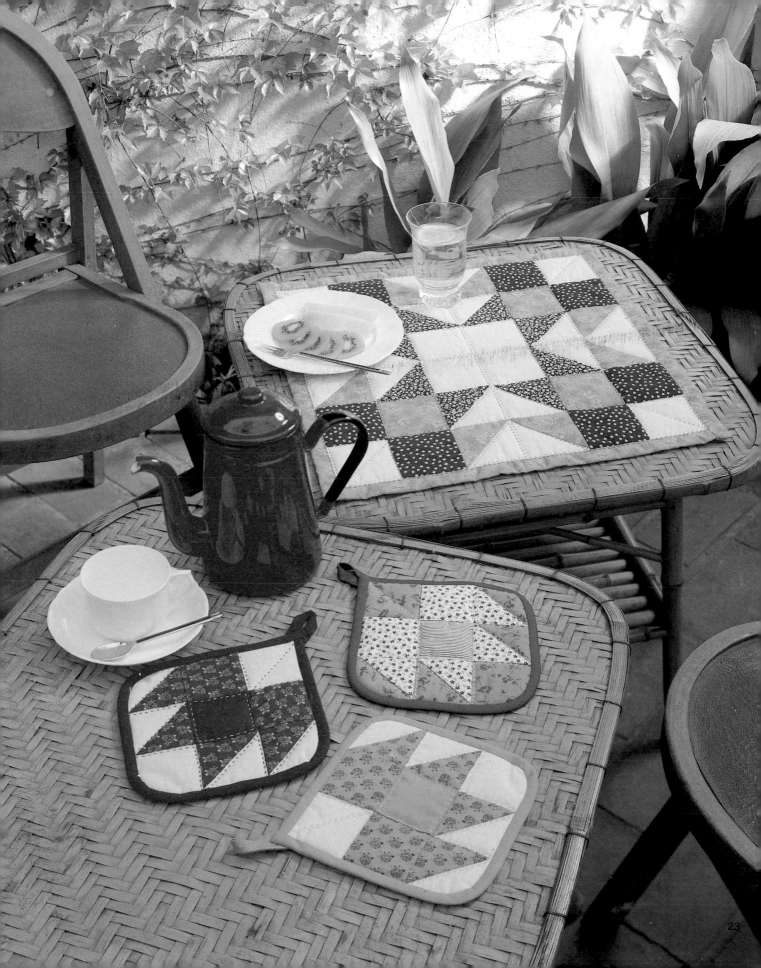

NINE-PATCH STAR AND DOUBLE BUTTERFLY
Bags and Pen Cases, Vanity Bags and Eyeglass Cases

Two simple but interesting Nine-Patch arrangements.

Bag
For each bag, you will need:
½ yard of 45-inch wide prequilted fabric
¾ yard of 45-inch wide print cotton (a)
  (includes pocket backing, binding, and patches)
Scraps of print or solid cotton (b)
  (or ⅛ yard if purchased)
5½-inch square of fleece type batting
Finished size: 9 inches × 10 inches with
  8-inch flap

Pen Case
For each pen case, you will need:
¼ yard of 45-inch wide print or solid cotton
  (includes backing and patches)
¼ yard of 45-inch wide print or solid cotton
⅛ yard of fleece type batting
¾ yard of matching regular bias tape
Medium-size snap
Cotton thread to match (b)
Finished size: 3½ inches × 6¾ inches with
  2¾-inch flap

Vanity Bag
For each vanity bag, you will need:
¼ yard of 45-inch wide cotton print (a)
  (includes backing and patches)
⅛ yard of 45-inch wide print or solid cotton (b)
Scrap of print or solid cotton (c)
¼ yard of fleece type batting
¾ yard of matching wide bias tape
Matching 7-inch zipper
Matching cotton thread
Finished size: 4¼ inches × 7¼ inches

Eyeglass Case
For each eyeglass case, you will need:
Scraps of print and solid cottons (a) and (b)
  (includes back piece, backing, and patches)
  (or ⅛ yard of each if purchased)
⅛ yard fleece type batting
1 yard matching regular bias tape
2 medium-size snaps
Matching cotton thread
Finished size: 4⅝ inches × 7⅝ inches

Patterns of the patches used (actual size)
Add ¼-inch seam allowance.

To make up
Join in sequences (1)–(3)

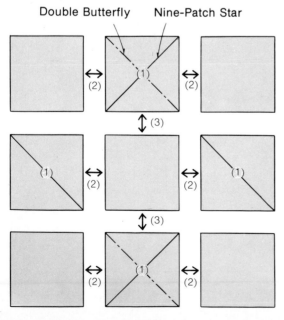

Double Butterfly   Nine-Patch Star

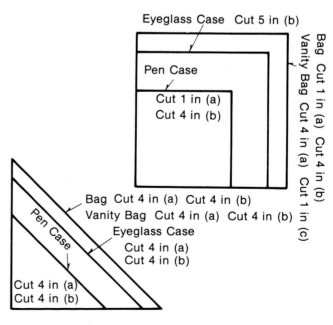

Eyeglass Case Cut 5 in (b)

Pen Case

Cut 1 in (a)
Cut 4 in (b)

Bag Cut 1 in (a) Cut 4 in (b)
Vanity Bag Cut 4 in (a) Cut 1 in (c)

Bag Cut 4 in (a) Cut 4 in (b)
Vanity Bag Cut 4 in (a) Cut 4 in (b)
Eyeglass Case
Cut 4 in (a)
Cut 4 in (b)

Pen Case

Cut 4 in (a)
Cut 4 in (b)

Continued on page 78

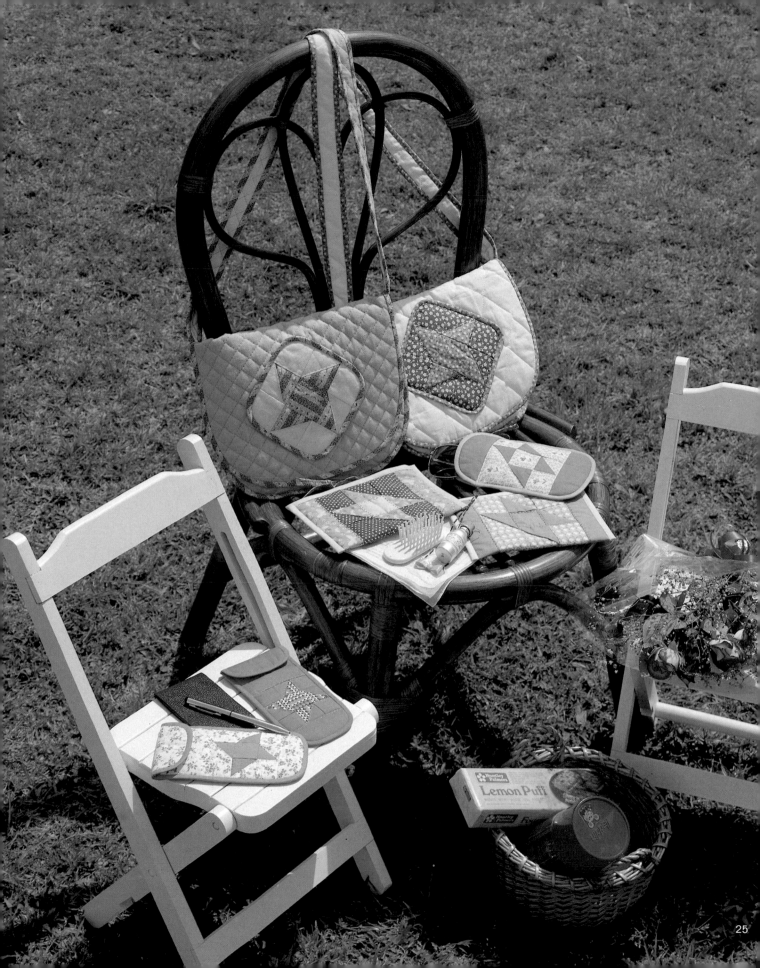

BISCUIT PATCHWORK
Crib Quilt

Baby's quilt made from soft, stuffed squares in pastel colors.

You will need:

3½ yards of 45-inch wide gray-green dressweight cotton (includes binding, lining, and some top pieces)
3¼ yards of 45-inch wide pink dressweight cotton (includes all backing pieces and some top pieces)
⅝ yard of 45-inch wide pink print cotton
⅝ yard of 45-inch wide pink-and-white print cotton
Synthetic filler
Matching cotton thread
Finished size: 58½ inches × 48½ inches

Chart of Measurements
¼-size pattern guides
Add ¼-inch seam allowance

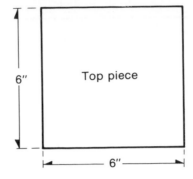

6" | Top piece | 6"

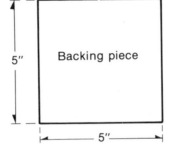

5" | Backing piece | 5"

To make up

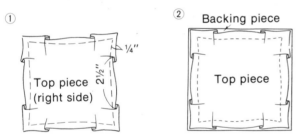

① Top piece (right side) ¼" 2½"

Make ¼-inch pleats on top piece to bring it down in size to fit 5-inch backing piece. Pin or baste pleats in place.

② Backing piece / Top piece

With wrong sides together, sew top pieces to backing pieces. Leave 2 inches open, stuff lightly and continue to sew around.

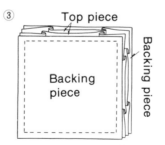

③ Top piece / Backing piece / Backing piece

With right sides together, seam patches to form rows of 9, using zipper or cording foot on the machine, and allowing ¼-inch seam. (Refer to the chart on page 80 for color arrangement.)

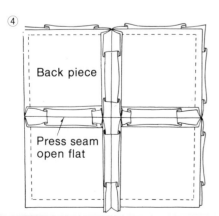

④ Back piece / Press seam open flat

Seam the rows together, making sure that seams meet at intersections.

Continued on page 80

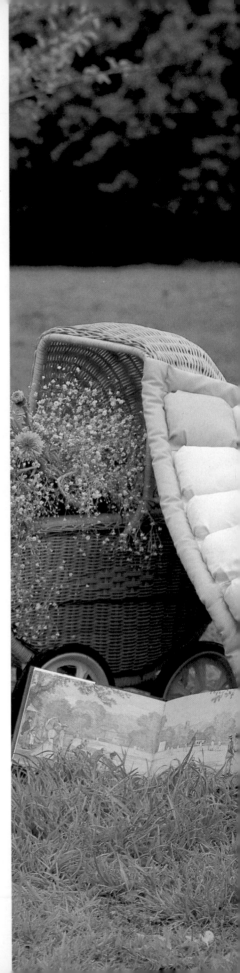

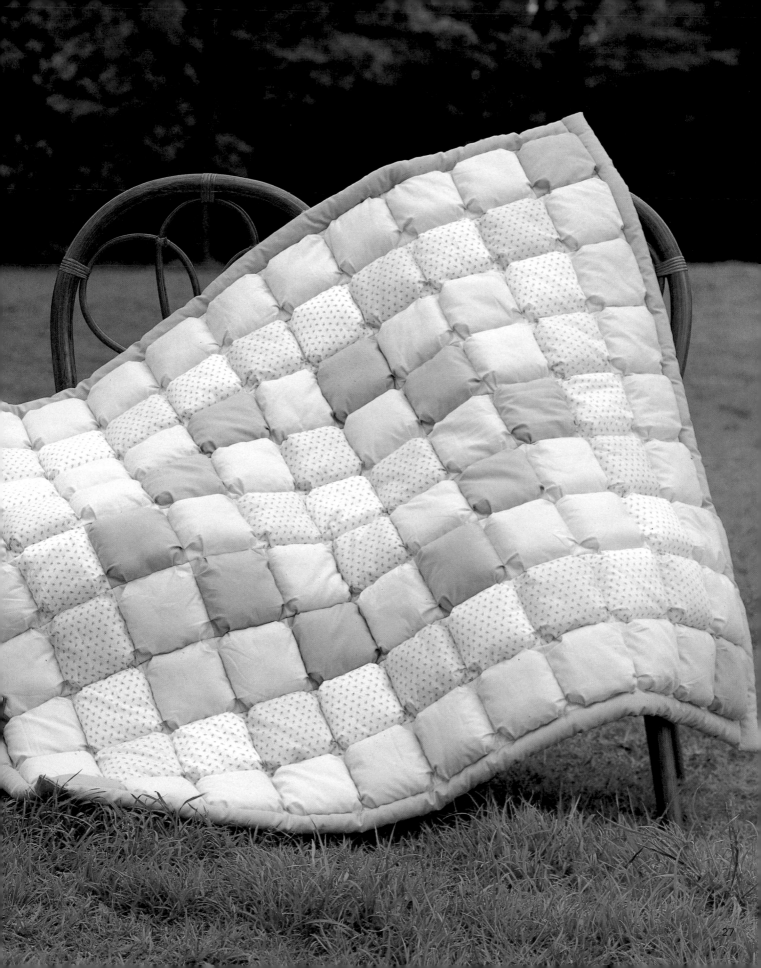

DOUBLE WEDDING RING
Crib or Lap Quilt

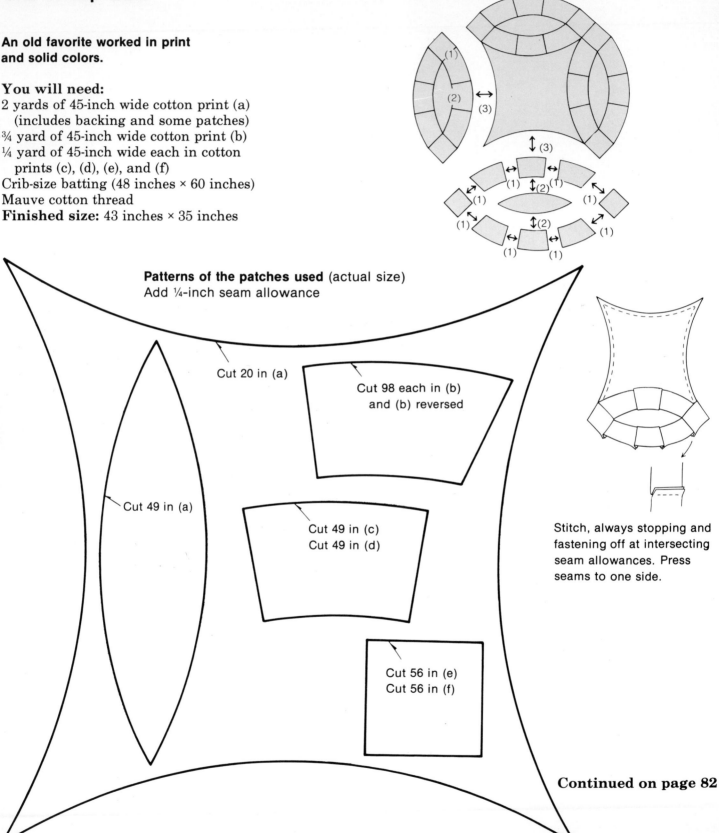

**An old favorite worked in print
and solid colors.**

You will need:
2 yards of 45-inch wide cotton print (a)
   (includes backing and some patches)
¾ yard of 45-inch wide cotton print (b)
¼ yard of 45-inch wide each in cotton
   prints (c), (d), (e), and (f)
Crib-size batting (48 inches × 60 inches)
Mauve cotton thread
Finished size: 43 inches × 35 inches

To make up
Join in sequences (1)–(3)

Patterns of the patches used (actual size)
Add ¼-inch seam allowance

Cut 20 in (a)

Cut 98 each in (b)
and (b) reversed

Cut 49 in (a)

Cut 49 in (c)
Cut 49 in (d)

Cut 56 in (e)
Cut 56 in (f)

Stitch, always stopping and
fastening off at intersecting
seam allowances. Press
seams to one side.

Continued on page 82

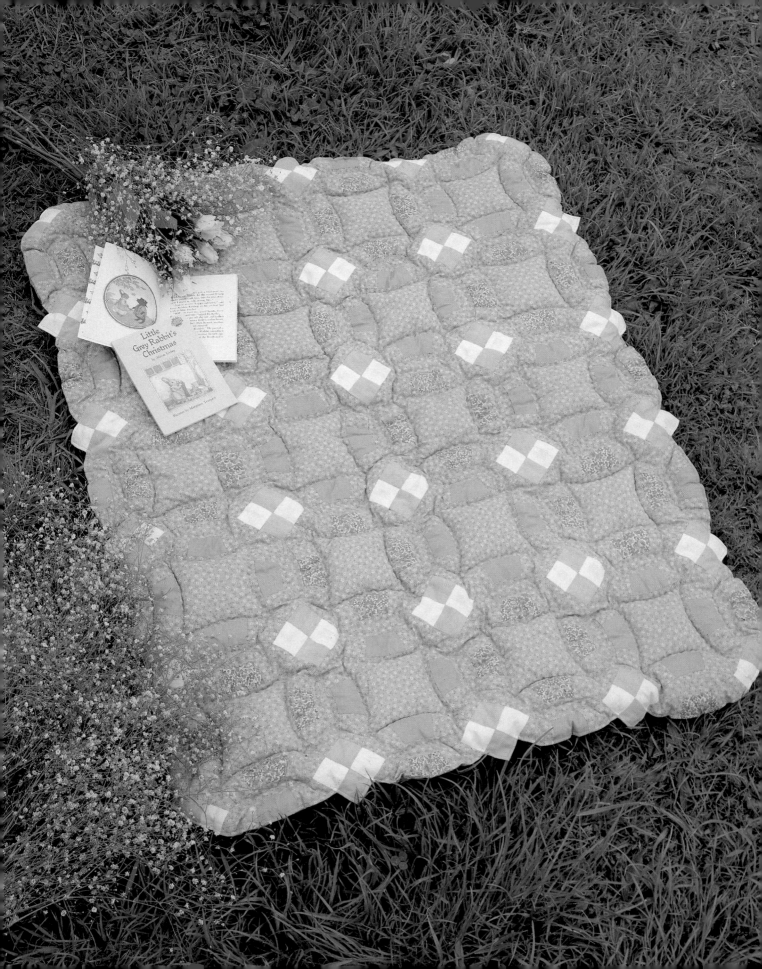

CATHEDRAL WINDOW
Cushion and Pincushions

**The insets of print fabric in
the folded squares of solid color
form the Cathedral Window effects.**

Cushion
You will need:
1¾ yards of 45-inch wide unbleached muslin
  for foundation (includes pillow back)
¼ yard of red print cotton for decoration
20-inch square inner cushion
18-inch zipper
Matching cotton thread
Finished size: 18¼ inches × 18¼ inches

Pincushions
For each pincushion, you will need:
¼ yard of 45-inch wide solid color cotton for foundation
½ yard of matching corded piping for pink pincushion
Scraps of blending print cotton for decoration
Small amount of synthetic filler
Matching cotton thread
Finished size: 4¼ inches × 4¼ inches

Chart of Measurements

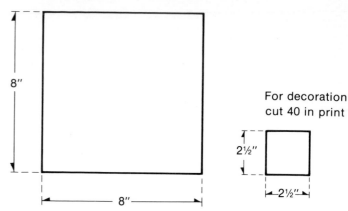

Cushion
For foundation cut 25 in unbleached muslin

8″ × 8″

For decoration
cut 40 in print
2½″ × 2½″

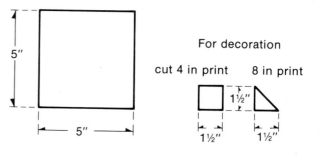

Pincushions
For foundation cut 4 in solid color

5″ × 5″

For decoration

cut 4 in print   8 in print
1½″ × 1½″   1½″

To make up

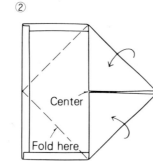

① Solid color foundation square
Turn under ¼ inch around edge.

② Center / Fold here

③ Sew centers together firmly by hand.

④ Fold here
Turn new corners over, fold as before.

⑤ Secure the center firmly with cross-stitch.

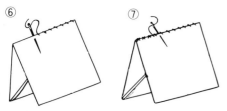

⑥ ⑦ With right sides together, overcast
pieces edge to edge. Work in rows,
taking only a small bit of the edge.
Work overcast back in the
other direction for added strength.

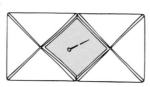

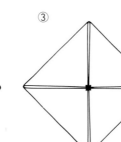

⑧ Lay decorative print
squares in the squares
on the right side
of the joined pieces.

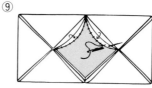

⑨ Turn folded edges of
foundation squares over
the edges of the print
squares. Secure with
blindstitch.

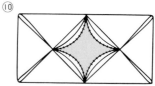

⑩ Each side of each shape
should curve evenly.

30

Continued on page 81

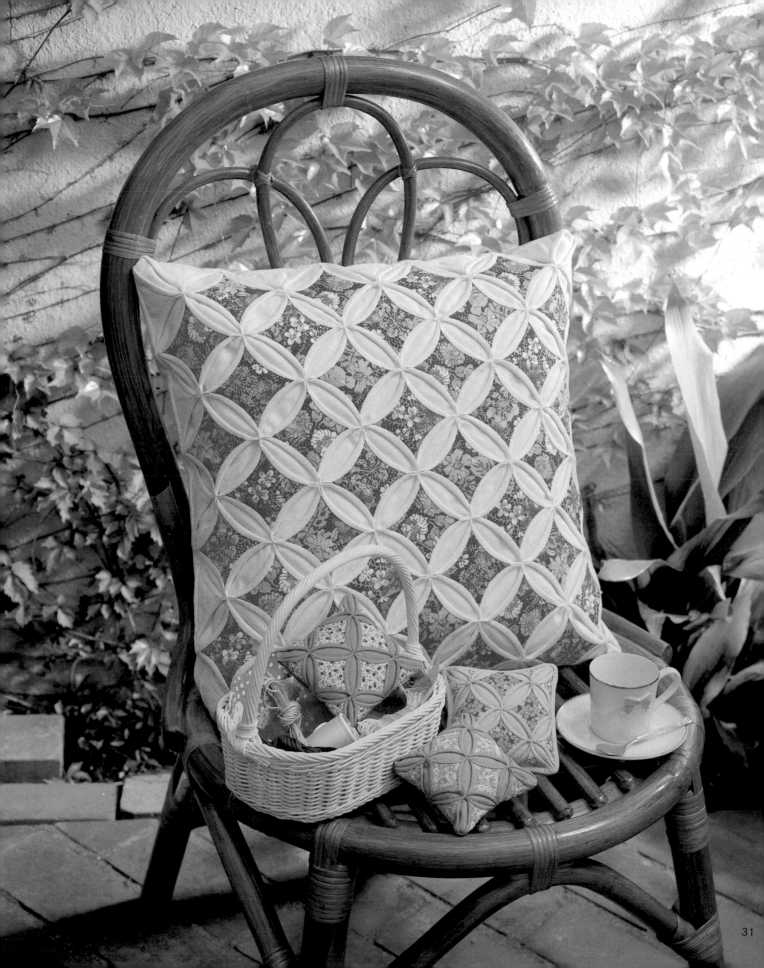

SCHOOLHOUSE
Bags

These bags, decorated with the traditional Schoolhouse design, are fun for children.

For each bag, you will need:
½ yard of 45-inch wide prequilted off-white fabric
Scraps of print and solid cottons (a), (b), (c), (d), and (e)
  (or ⅛ yard of each if purchased)
⅝ yard of 1¼-inch wide unbleached cotton handle
  webbing
¾ yard of matching regular bias tape (a)
Finished size: 10 inches × 12 inches with 2-inch
  mitered base.

Patterns for appliqué
Add ¼-inch seam allowance

To make up
Join in sequences (1)–(5). At stage (1) appliqué window, door, and chimneys in place.

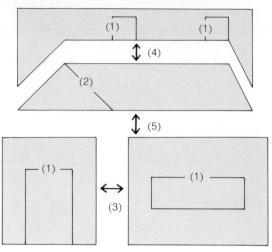

Continued on page 82

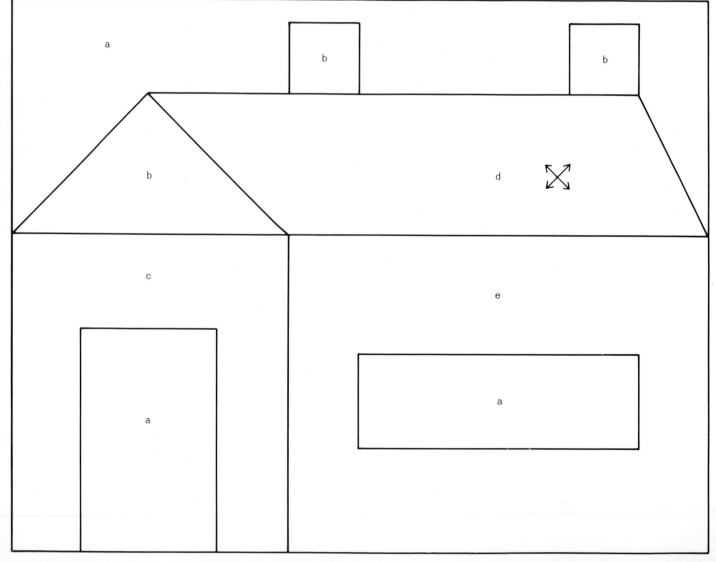

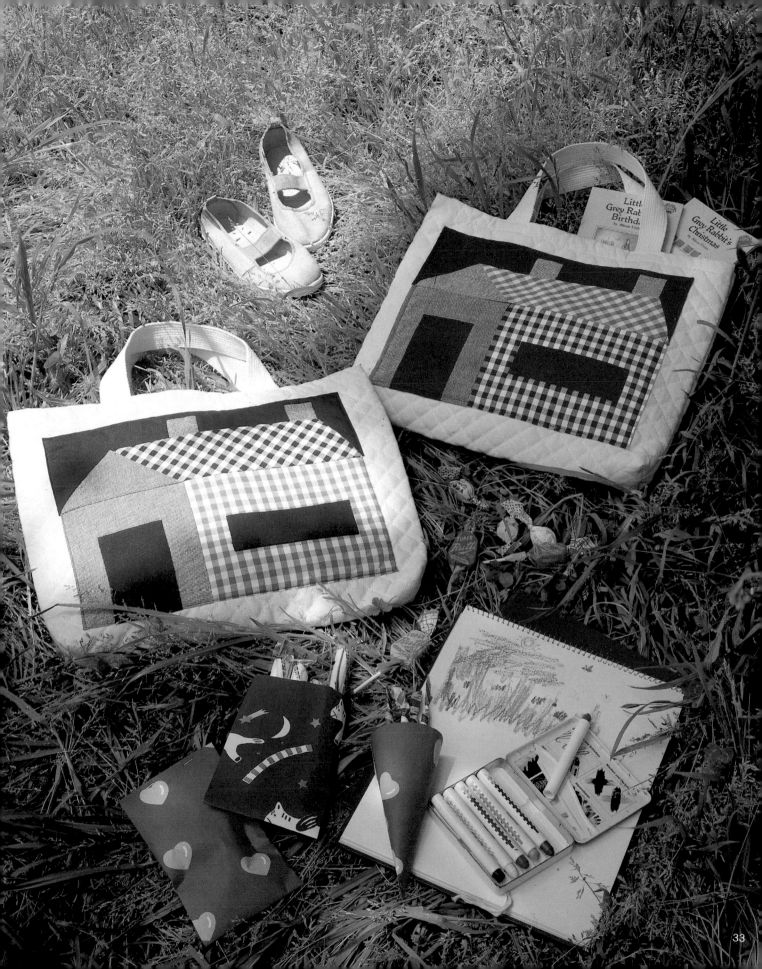

TULIP
Miniature Cushions

**A triangle and diamonds make
a stylized tulip.**

For 3 cushions, you will need:
½ yard of 45-inch wide pale green cotton
  (includes cushion backs and patches)
½ yard of unbleached muslin
Scraps of contrasting cotton (a)
  (or ⅛ yard if purchased)
1 bag of synthetic filler
Finished size: 8 inches × 8 inches

Patterns of the patches used (actual size)
Add ¼-inch seam allowance

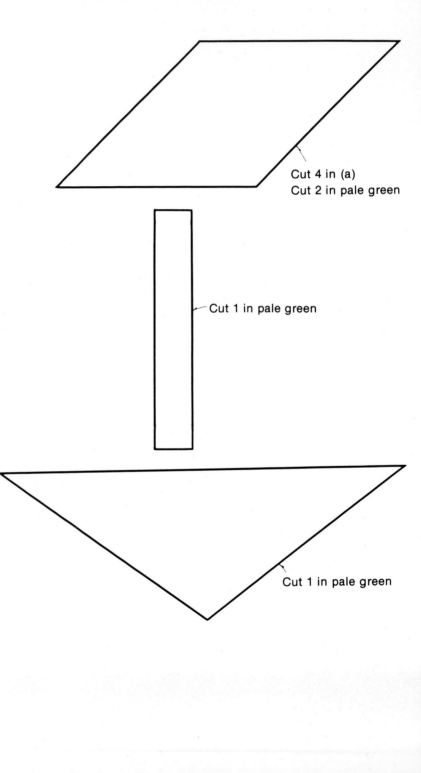

Cut 4 in (a)
Cut 2 in pale green

Cut 1 in pale green

Cut 1 in pale green

To make up
Join in sequences (1)–(2)

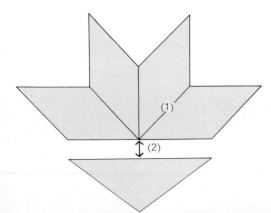

(1)

(2)

Continued on page 75

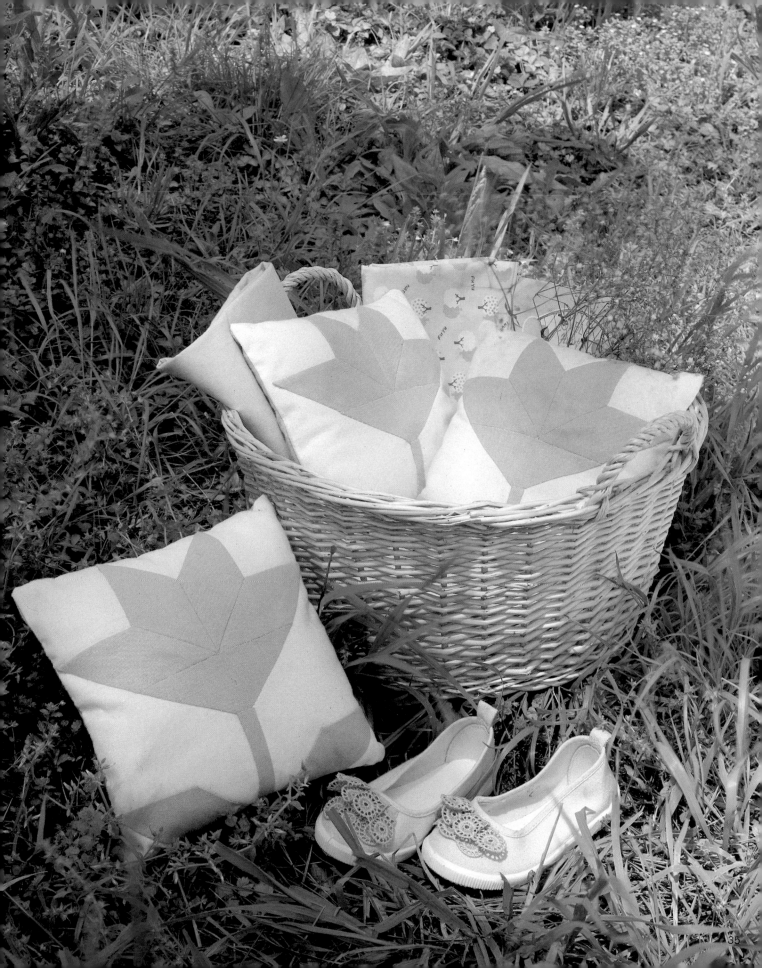

BOY AND GIRL
Toaster Cover, Tea Cozy, and Cushions

These designs can be scaled up in size, as suggested, to fit the pieces shown, or used same size on children's clothes.

Toaster Cover
You will need:
⅝ yard of 45-inch wide lime green cotton
Scraps of yellow and navy blue solid color,
   and print cottons (a), (b), and (c)
⅝ yard of 45-inch wide very thin backing
⅝ yard of 45-inch wide colored lining (optional)
2½ yards of dark green corded piping
1 yard of dark green regular bias tape (optional)
Brown, red, green, pink, and aqua six-strand
   embroidery floss
Finished size: 11 inches × 7½ inches × 6 inches deep

Tea Cozy
You will need:
⅜ yard of 45-inch wide lime green cotton

Scraps of yellow, white, moss green, red and orange
   solid color, and print cottons (a) and (b)
⅜ yard of 45-inch wide lining to match any of the
   above
⅜ yard of fleece type batting (used double if preferred)
Small amount of synthetic filler
Brown, red, orange, yellow, and white six-strand
   embroidery floss
Finished size: 13 inches × 9½ inches

Cushions
For each cushion, you will need:
(Materials apply to both cushions, except where
   parentheses indicate alternative for girl)
½ yard of 45-inch wide blue (red) print cotton
¼ yard of 45-inch wide white cotton
Scraps of navy blue (red polka dot) and yellow
   solid color cottons
1 yard of ⅝-inch wide washable ribbon or tape
   in blue (red)
9-inch zipper to match print
1-inch thick form cushion (if larger than finished
   size, it can be cut to shape)
Brown, red (green, yellow) six-strand embroidery floss
Finished size: 12 inches × 13 inches

Appliqué Design   Add ¼-inch seam allowance

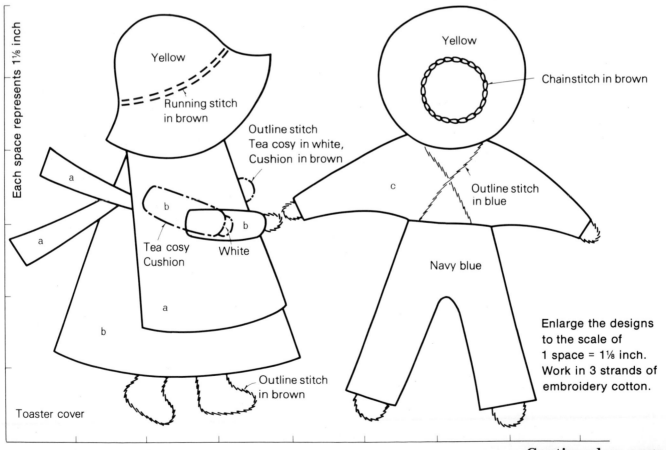

Each space represents 1⅛ inch

Yellow
Running stitch
in brown
Outline stitch
Tea cosy in white,
Cushion in brown
a
b
b
b
a
Tea cosy
Cushion
White
a
b
Outline stitch
in brown
Toaster cover

Yellow
Chainstitch in brown
c
Outline stitch
in blue
Navy blue
Enlarge the designs
to the scale of
1 space = 1⅛ inch.
Work in 3 strands of
embroidery cotton.

36

Continued on page 83

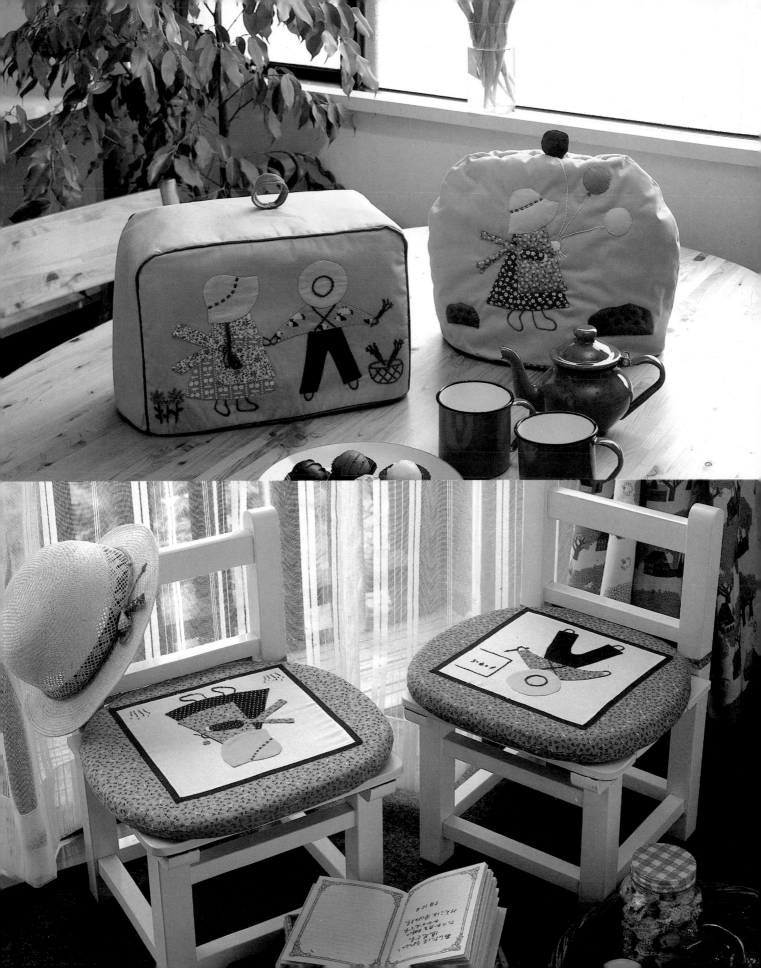

CAROLINA LILY
Cushion

An abstract lily design composed of diamonds and triangles in a bold color scheme.

You will need:

½ yard of 45-inch wide black-and-white polka dot print (includes cushion back and 4 corner pieces)

½ yard of 45-inch wide black dressweight cotton (includes backing and some patches)

Scraps of green and red solid color, and red-and-white polka dot cottons (or ⅛ yard of each if purchased)

½ yard of fleece type batting

14-inch black zipper

16-inch square inner cushion

Matching cotton thread

Finished size: 16¼ inches × 16¼ inches

To make up

Join in sequences (1)–(10)
At stages (7) and (8) appliqué
stems and buds with blindstitch

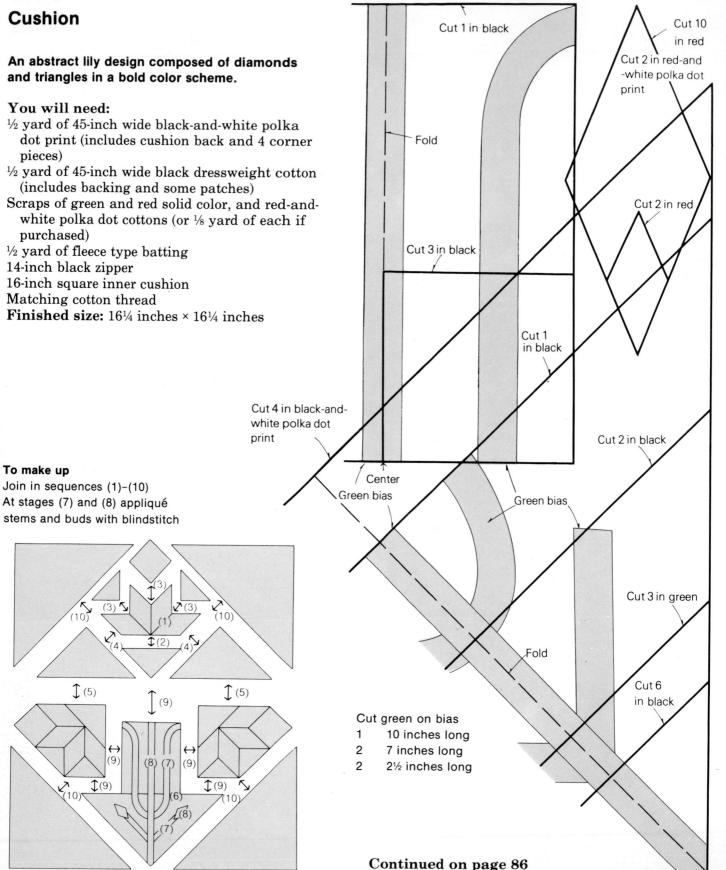

Patterns of the patches used (actual size)
Add ¼-inch seam allowance

Cut 1 in black

Cut 10 in red

Cut 2 in red-and-white polka dot print

Fold

Cut 3 in black

Cut 2 in red

Cut 1 in black

Cut 4 in black-and-white polka dot print

Cut 2 in black

Center
Green bias

Green bias

Cut 3 in green

Fold

Cut 6 in black

Cut green on bias
1   10 inches long
2   7 inches long
2   2½ inches long

Continued on page 86

38

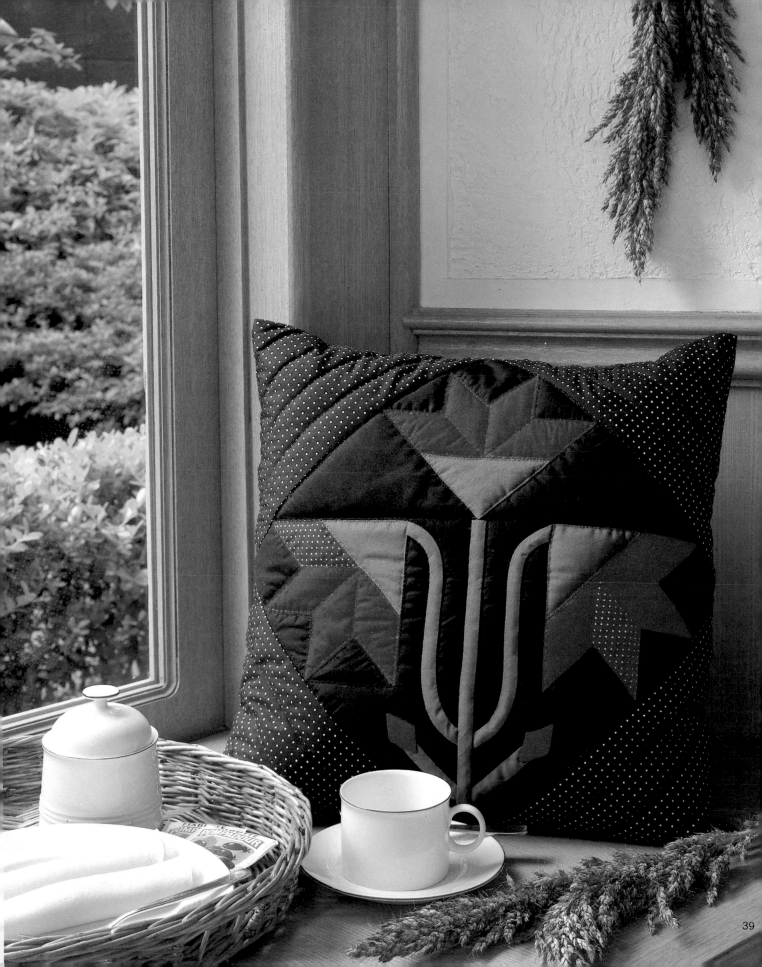

TWO FLOWER BASKET DESIGNS
Patchwork Picture and Cushion

The baskets are composed of geometric pieces. The appliquéd handle completes the picture.

Patchwork Picture
You will need:
¼ yard of 45-inch-wide blue dressweight cotton
   (includes backing and some patches)
⅛ yard of 45-inch wide moss green print cotton
¼ yard of fleece type batting
Blue cotton thread
Do-it-yourself framing from art supply store
Finished size: 7½ inches × 7½ inches

Cushion
You will need:
½ yard of 45-inch wide print cotton (a)
Scraps of brown and yellow solid color cottons
   (b) and (c) (or ⅛ yard of each if purchased)
¼ yard of 45-inch wide cotton print (d)
14-inch zipper to match (a)
1-inch thick foam cushion (if larger than
   finished size, it can be cut to shape)
Matching cotton thread
Finished size: 16 inches × 18 inches

To make up (patchwork picture)
Join in sequences (1)–(7)
Turn under seam allowance on (6)
and blindstitch

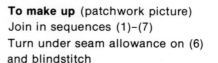

Patterns of the patches used (actual size)
Add ¼-inch seam allowance

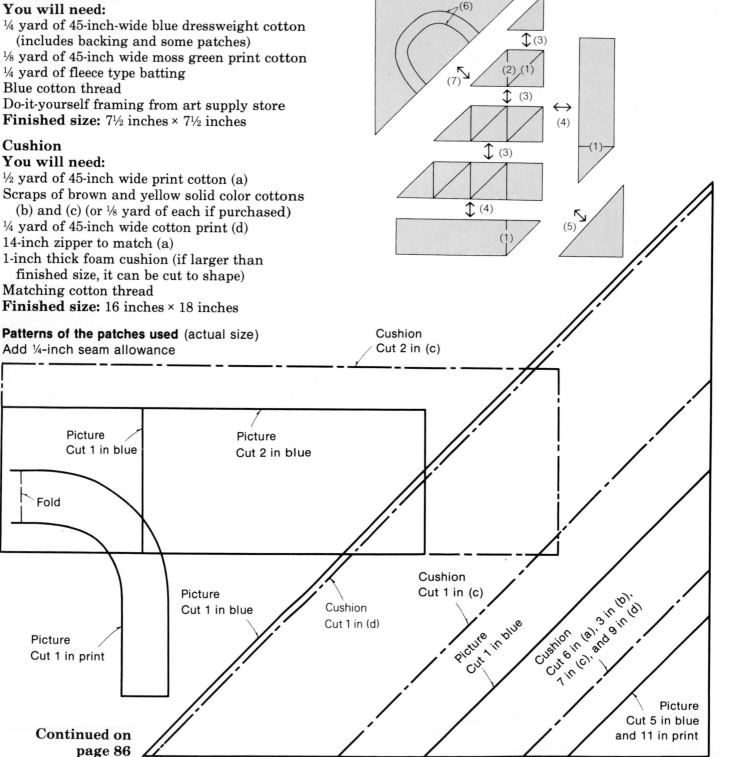

Cushion
Cut 2 in (c)

Picture
Cut 1 in blue

Picture
Cut 2 in blue

Fold

Picture
Cut 1 in blue

Cushion
Cut 1 in (d)

Cushion
Cut 1 in (c)

Picture
Cut 1 in blue

Cushion
Cut 6 in (a), 3 in (b),
7 in (c), and 9 in (d)

Picture
Cut 1 in print

Picture
Cut 5 in blue
and 11 in print

Continued on page 86

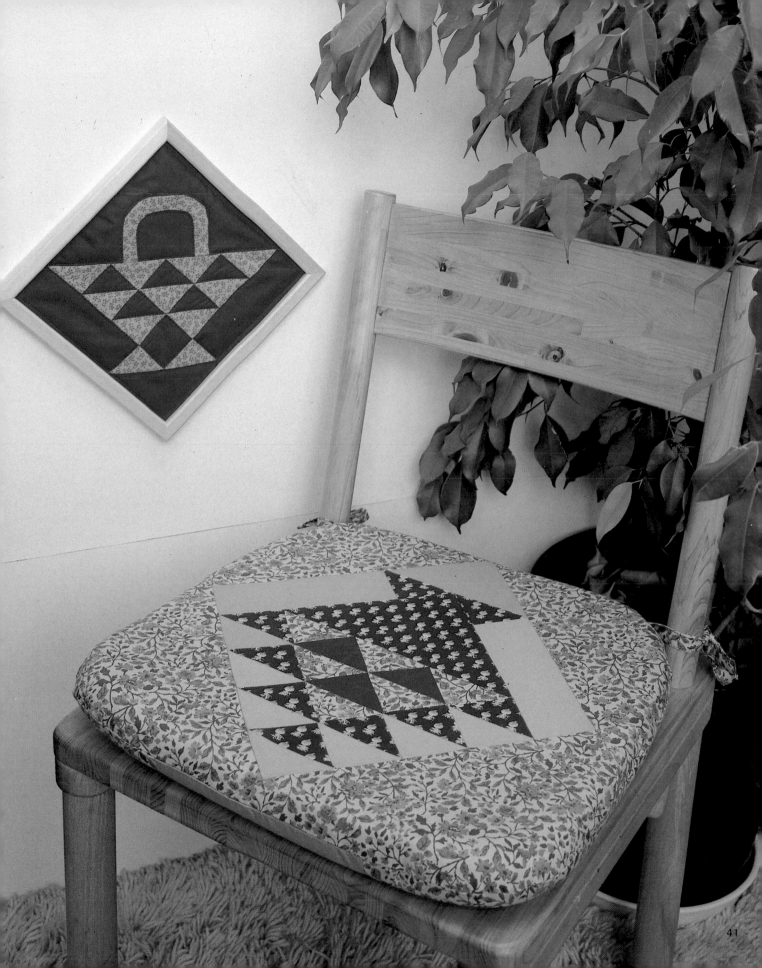

BABY BLOCKS
Crib Quilt

This design is composed of diamonds and hexagons in print and solid color cottons, arranged to give a three-dimensional effect. It can be made by the paper-liner method (see page 101) or by skilled hand or machine piecing.

You will need:
3¾ yards of 45-inch wide pale pink dressweight cotton (includes backing and border)
1¾ yards of 45-inch wide unbleached muslin
½ yard of 45-inch wide yellow dressweight cotton
1⅞ yards of 45-inch wide rust dressweight cotton
¼ yard of 45-inch wide lime green dressweight cotton
Scrap of gold dressweight cotton (or ⅛ yard if purchased)
⅜ yard of 45-inch wide print cottons (a), (c), and (e)
⅛ yard of 45-inch wide print cotton (f)
Scraps of print cottons (b), (d), (g), and (h) (or ⅛ yard if purchased)
Twin-size batting (39 inches × 75 inches)
Off-white cotton thread
Finished size: 67 inches × 44½ inches

To make up
Join in sequences (1)–(5)

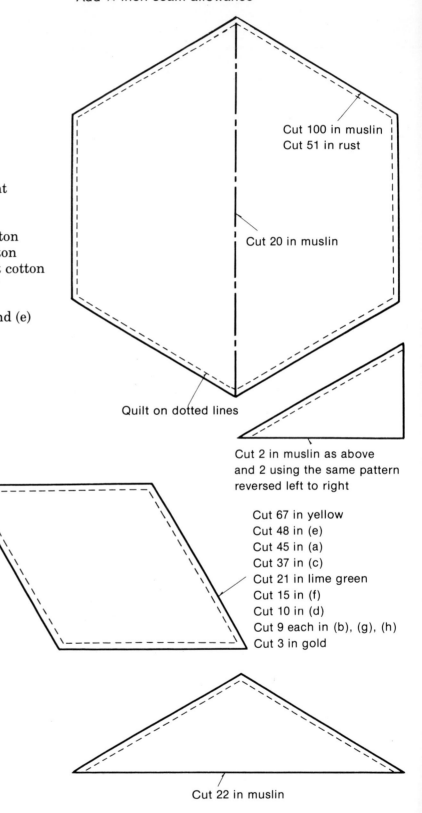

Cut 100 in muslin
Cut 51 in rust

Cut 20 in muslin

Quilt on dotted lines

Cut 2 in muslin as above and 2 using the same pattern reversed left to right

Cut 67 in yellow
Cut 48 in (e)
Cut 45 in (a)
Cut 37 in (c)
Cut 21 in lime green
Cut 15 in (f)
Cut 10 in (d)
Cut 9 each in (b), (g), (h)
Cut 3 in gold

Cut 22 in muslin

42

Continued on page 93

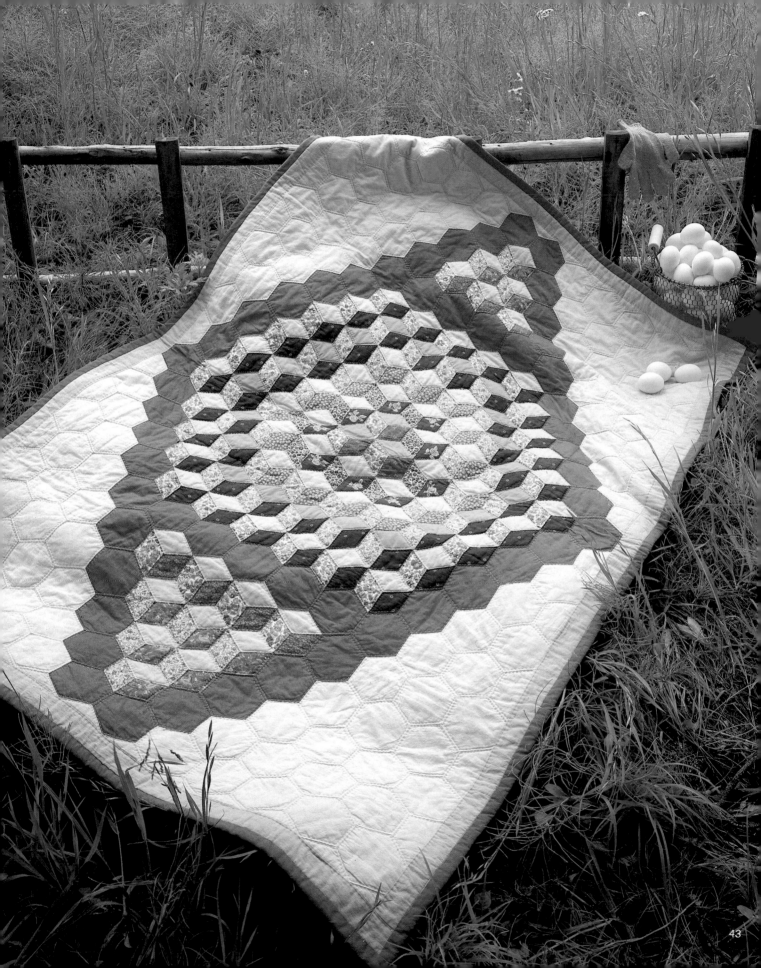

KALEIDOSCOPE
Twin-Bed Quilt

(**For a longer quilt to be used as a bedspread, add two or three rows to the end. For double-bed size add one or two rows to the side.**) **Two triangles form the basis of this colorful design. By alternating white, light, and dark patches, a kaleidoscopic effect is achieved.**

You will need:
1½ yards of 45-inch wide white dressweight cotton
For 400 pieces a total of 1¾ yards of 45-inch wide light-colored cottons (scrap)
For 400 pieces a total of 1¾ yards of 45-inch wide dark-colored cottons (scrap)
5½ yards of cream-colored dressweight cotton (includes backing and binding)
Double-size quilt batting (80 inches × 97 inches)
White cotton thread
Finished size: 72½ inches × 72½ inches

To make up
Join in sequences (1) and (2)

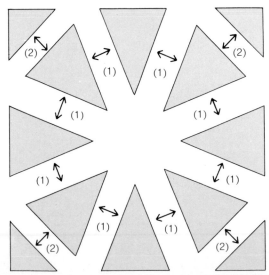

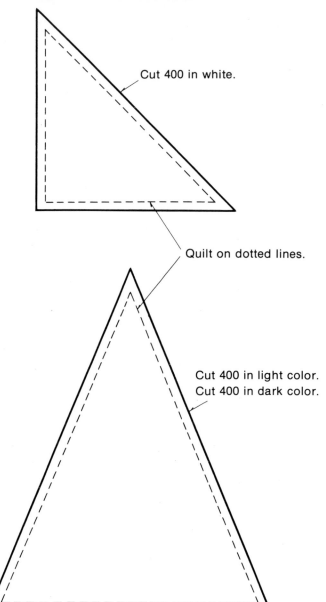

Patterns of the patches used (actual size)
Add ¼-inch seam allowance.

Cut 400 in white.

Quilt on dotted lines.

Cut 400 in light color.
Cut 400 in dark color.

Continued on page 83

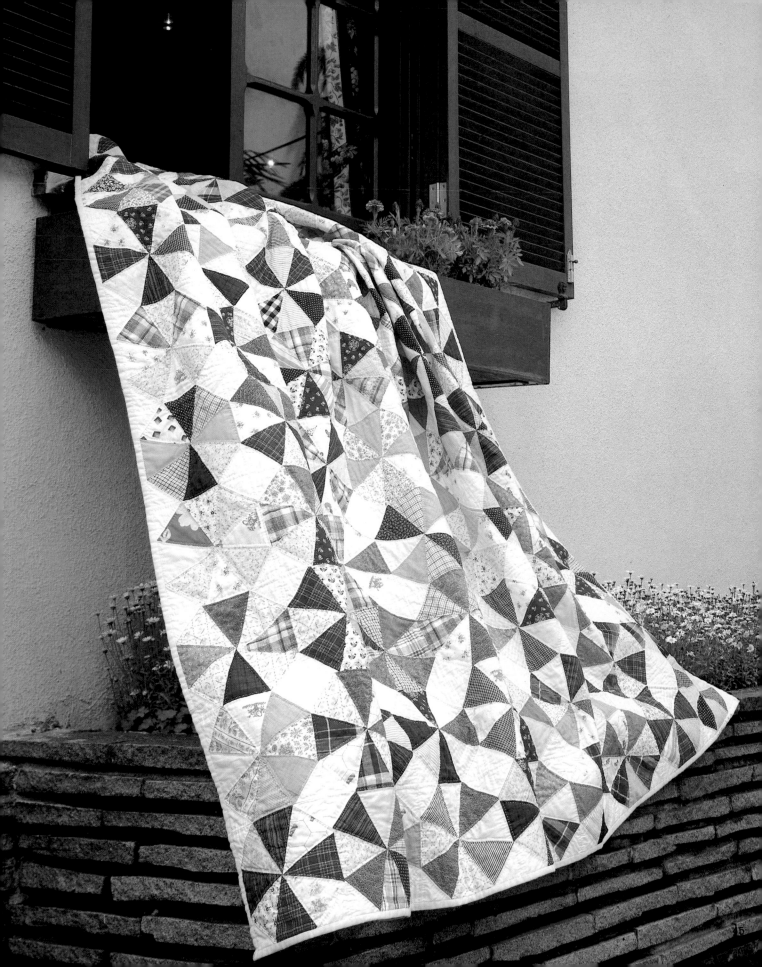

WINDMILL
Table Mat and Tray Cloth

Squares of Windmill patchwork are alternated with squares of Sunflower quilting on plain fabric.

Tray Cloth
You will need:
¼ yard of 45-inch wide unbleached muslin
Scraps of solid red and red checked cotton
  (or ⅛ yard of each if purchased)
⅜ yard of 45-inch wide moss green dressweight
  cotton (includes backing and binding)
⅜ yard of fleece type batting
Red cotton thread
Finished size: 12¼ inches × 12¼ inches

Table Mat
You will need:
½ yard of 45-inch wide unbleached muslin
20 scraps of colored dressweight cottons
  (or ⅛ yard of all one color if purchased)
⅝ yard of 45-inch wide olive green dressweight cotton
  (includes backing, binding, and some patches)
⅝ yard of fleece type batting
Natural cotton thread
Finished size: 18¼ inches × 18¼ inches

To make up
Join in sequences (1)–(3)

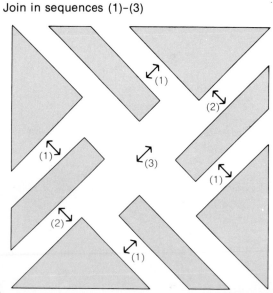

Patterns of the patches used (actual size)
Add ¼-inch seam allowance

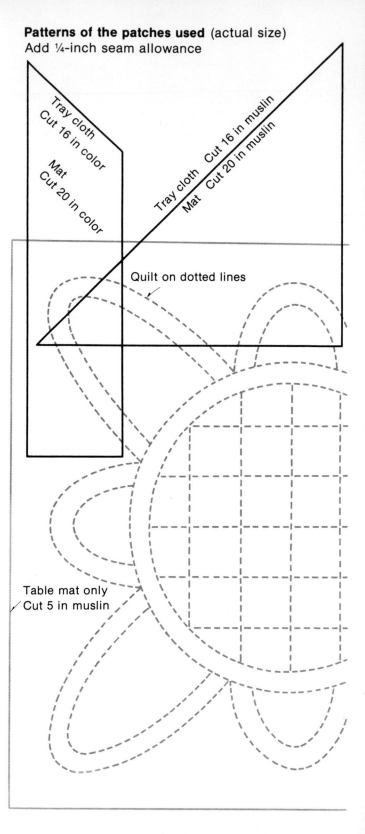

Tray cloth Cut 16 in color
Mat Cut 20 in color
Tray cloth Cut 16 in muslin
Mat Cut 20 in muslin
Quilt on dotted lines
Table mat only
Cut 5 in muslin

Continued on page 87

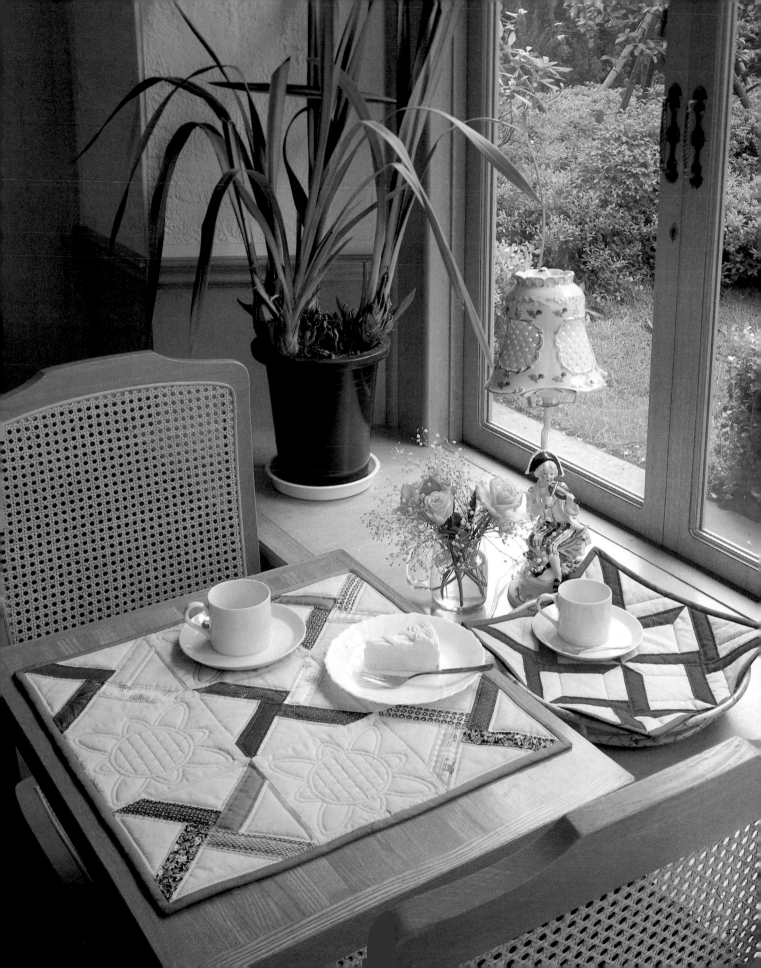

OLD MAID'S PUZZLE
Eyeglass Case

Triangles and squares combine to make
a variable and colorful puzzle design.

You will need:
Dressweight cottons (see pages 90–91)
8-inch scraps of fleece type batting
   (or ⅛ yard for several cases)
Matching cotton thread
Finished size: 7 inches × 3½ inches

Continued on page 90

To make up   Join in sequences (1)–(8)

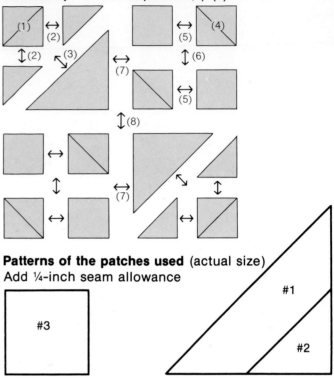

Patterns of the patches used (actual size)
Add ¼-inch seam allowance

#3

#1

#2

For cutting, see pages 90–91

SNOWBALL
Pincushions

An excellent beginner's project, incorporating
piecing and appliqué.

You will need:
Scraps or ¼ yard of firm cotton for main pieces
Scraps of print cottons (a), (b), (c), and (d)
Scraps or ¼ yard of fleece type batting
Small amounts of synthetic filler
Matching cotton thread
Finished size: 4¼ inches × 4¼ inches

Patterns of the patches used
(actual size)
Add ¼-inch seam allowance

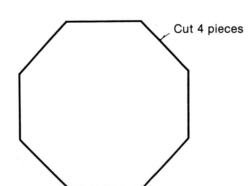

Cut 4 pieces

Join 4 pieces together first

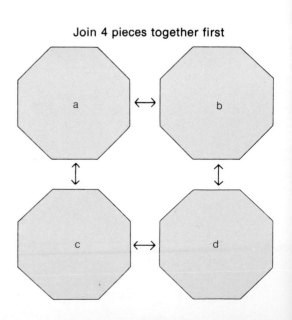

Continued on page 81

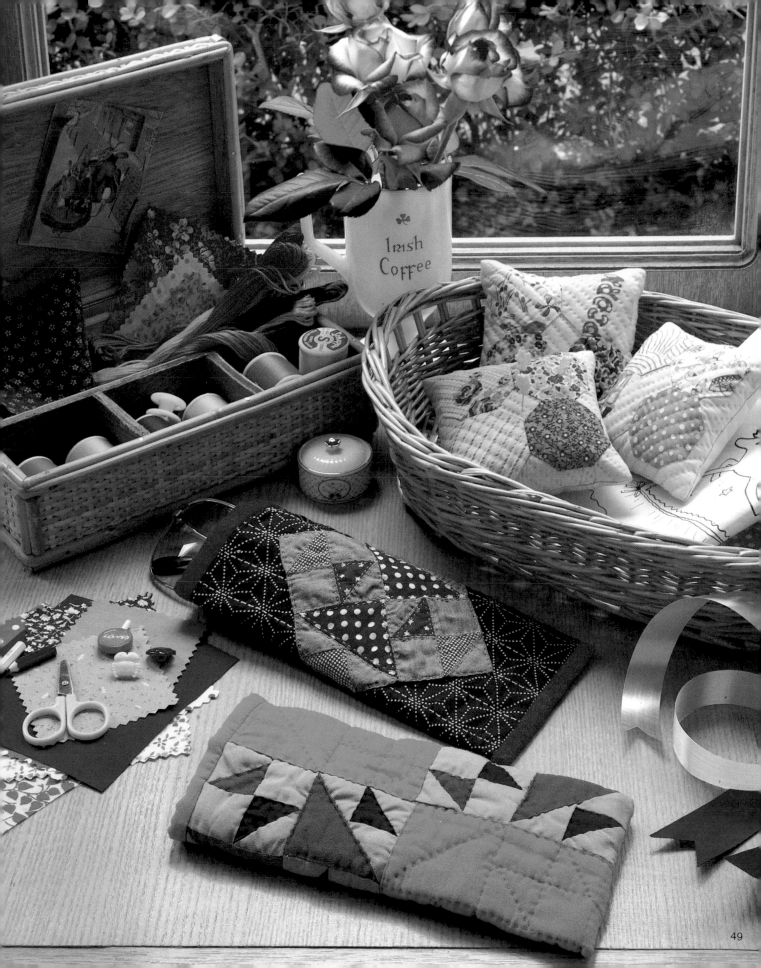

DRESDEN PLATE
Single-Bed Quilt and Sewing Pocket

(For a 78-inch wide quilt, add one more row of blocks and one more row of sash)
Floral prints are pieced around a center to make a traditional quilt design, which is appliquéd to the block.

Quilt
You will need:
4 yards of 45-inch wide blue dressweight cotton
6 yards of 45-inch wide red dressweight cotton
   (includes sashes, borders, backing, and some patches)
½ yard of 45-inch wide print cotton (a)
   (includes corner blocks and some patches)
¼ yard of 45-inch wide print cotton (b)
Scraps of print cottons (c), (d), (e), (f), (g), (h), (i), and (j)
   (or ⅛ yard of each if purchased)
Double-bed size batting (80 inches × 97 inches)
Red and blue cotton thread
Finished size: 63 inches × 93 inches

Sewing pocket
You will need:
½ yard of 45-inch wide print cotton (a)
   (includes front and back piece, binding, and motif center)
¼ yard of 45-inch wide print cotton (b)
   (includes both backing pieces and motif center rim)
Scraps of print cottons (c), (d), (e), and (f)
Scraps or ¼ yard of fleece type batting
Matching cotton thread
Finished size: 7 inches × 7 inches

To make up
Join (1) with running stitch.
Blindstitch at stages (2) and (3).

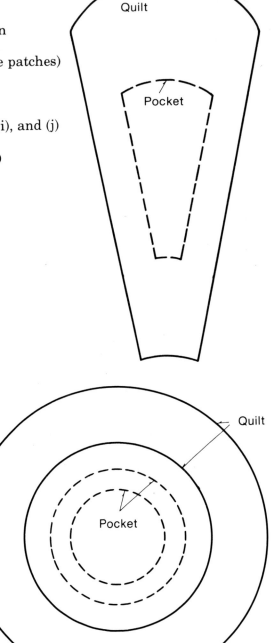

Patterns of the patches used
(actual size)
Add ¼-inch seam allowance

Quilt

Pocket

Quilt

Pocket

Continued on page 95

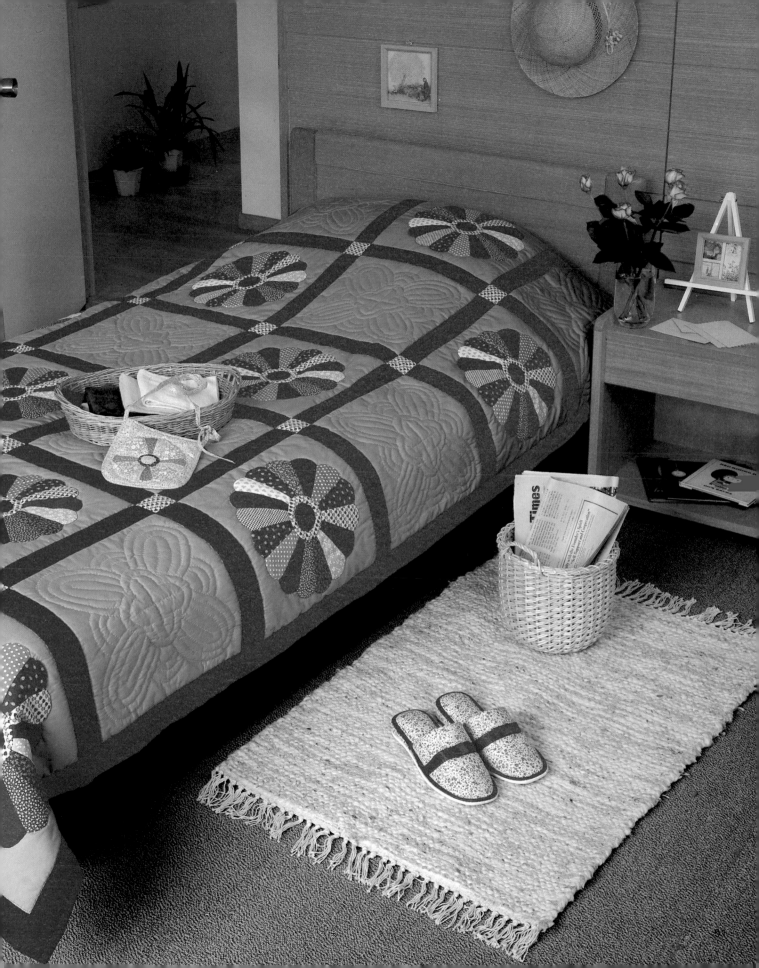

DUCK PADDLE
Mat and Small Purse

The Duck Paddle design is named for its shape and can be made in planned or scrap-bag fabrics.

Mat
You will need:
1¼ yards of 45-inch wide brown polka dot cotton (a)
   (includes binding, outer border (2), and some patches)
⅛ yard of 45-inch wide print cotton (b)
1 yard of 45-inch wide gold dressweight cotton (c)
   (includes backing, inner border (1), and some patches)
⅞ yard of fleece type batting
   (or 1⅝ yards if used double)
Matching cotton thread
Finished size: 36¾ inches × 26½ inches

Small Purse
You will need:
1 yard polka dot print cotton (a)
   (includes back piece, backing, shoulder strap,
   and some patches)
Scraps of navy solid color and light print cottons
   (b) and (c) (or ⅛ yard of each if purchased)
Scraps or ⅜ yard of fleece type batting
White cotton thread
Finished size: 9¼ inches × 9¼ inches

To make up
Join in sequences (1)-(5)

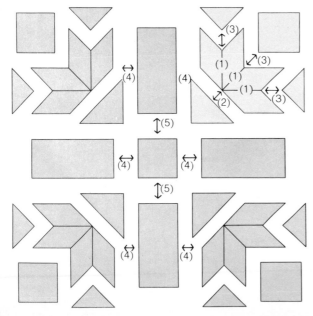

Add ¼-inch seam allowance

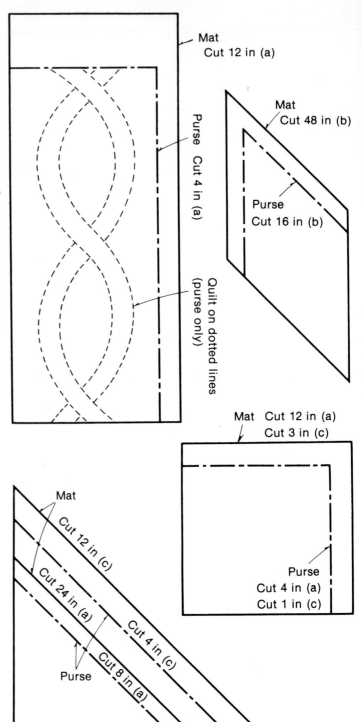

Mat
Cut 12 in (a)

Mat
Cut 48 in (b)

Purse Cut 4 in (a)

Purse
Cut 16 in (b)

Quilt on dotted lines
(purse only)

Mat   Cut 12 in (a)
Cut 3 in (c)

Mat
Cut 12 in (c)
Cut 24 in (a)
Cut 4 in (c)
Cut 8 in (a)

Purse

Purse
Cut 4 in (a)
Cut 1 in (c)

Total number of pieces cut

Continued on page 88

52

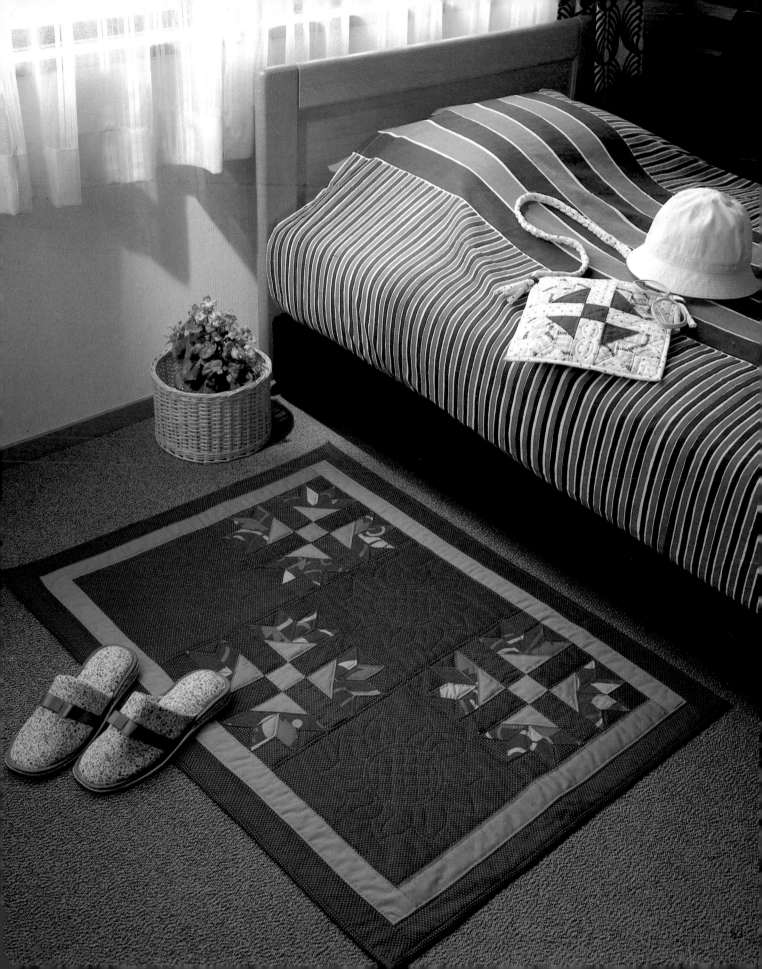

SAWTOOTH STAR
Runner and Placemat

One of many Star designs, this one based on the Four-Patch is simple enough for a beginner.

Placemats
For each mat you will need:
⅜ yard of 45-inch wide solid color dressweight
   cotton (a) (includes lining, border, and
   some patches)
Scraps of print cotton (b)
   (or ⅛ yard if purchased)
¼ yard of fleece type batting
Matching cotton thread
Finished size: 14¼ inches × 8⅛ inches

Runner
You will need:
⅜ yard of 45-inch wide black dressweight cotton
   (includes lining and borders)
⅛ yard of 45-inch wide gray dressweight cotton
⅛ yard each of gray print cottons (a) and (b)
¼ yard of fleece type batting
Matching cotton thread
Finished size: 32⅝ inches × 8⅛ inches

Patterns of the patches used (actual size)
Add ¼-inch seam allowance

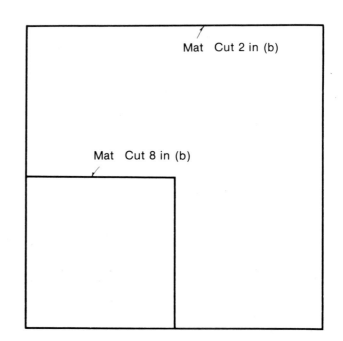

Mat   Cut 2 in (b)

Mat   Cut 8 in (b)

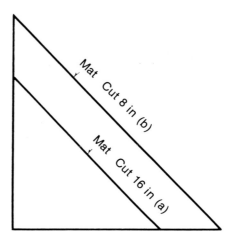

Mat   Cut 8 in (b)

Mat   Cut 16 in (a)

Note for runner: Reverse colors of (a) and (b) in alternate blocks. Cut smaller square and larger triangle in solid gray.

To make up
Join in sequences (1)–(4)

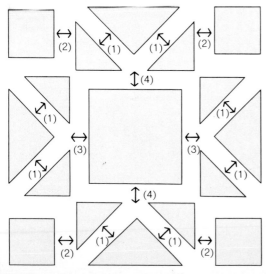

Continued on page 91

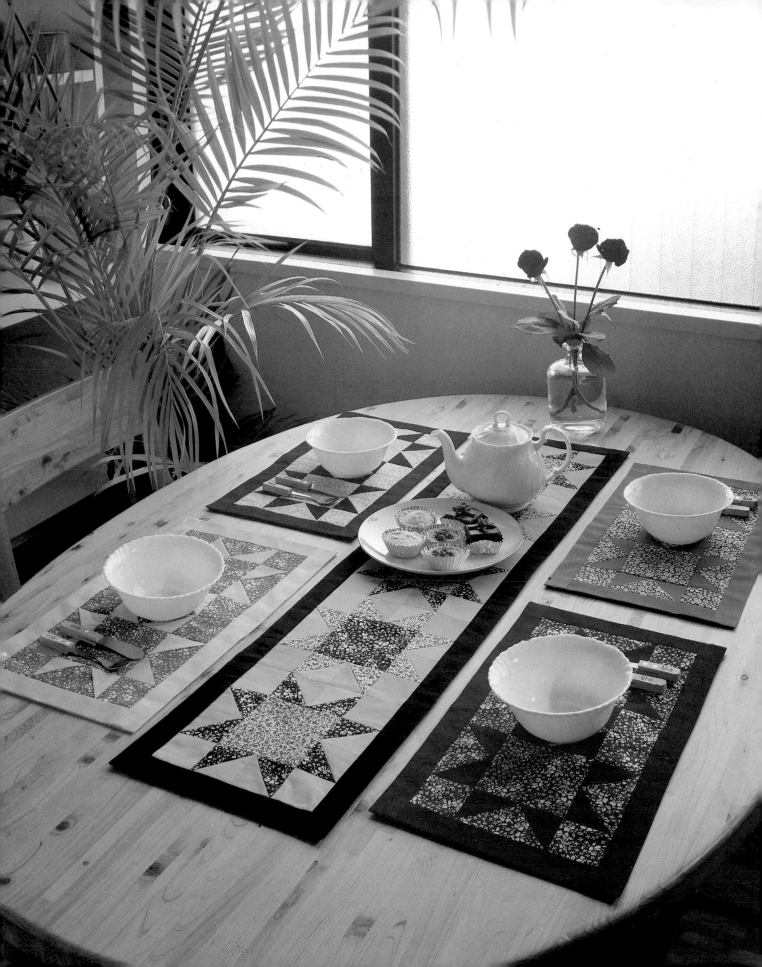

ROSE GARDEN
Potholder and Table Runner

An abstract Rose pattern, composed of triangles surrounding a central square.

Table Runner
You will need:
⅜ yard of 45-inch wide red dressweight cotton (a)
   (includes lining, border, sashes, and some patches)
Scraps of orange (c) and 2 print cottons (b) and (d)
   (or ⅛ yard of each if purchased)
¼ yard of fleece type batting
Matching cotton thread
Finished size: 31½ inches × 8¼ inches

Potholder
For each potholder, you will need:
⅜ yard of 45-inch wide solid color or print cotton (a)
   (includes lining, border, and some patches)
Scraps of print cotton (b)
   (or ⅛ yard if purchased)
¼ yard of fleece type batting (used double)
Matching cotton thread
Finished size: 7½ inches × 7½ inches

Patterns of the patches used (actual size)
Add ¼-inch seam allowance

For each block:

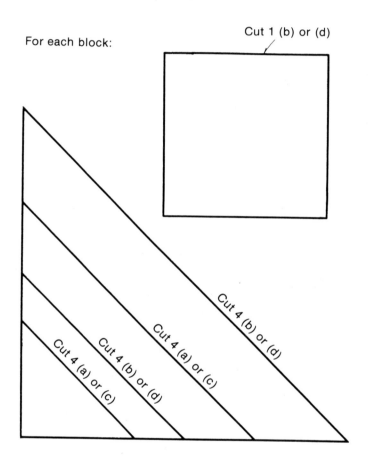

Cut 1 (b) or (d)
Cut 4 (b) or (d)
Cut 4 (a) or (c)
Cut 4 (b) or (d)
Cut 4 (a) or (c)

Note:
Follow color charts on page 92

To make up
Join in sequences (1)–(4)

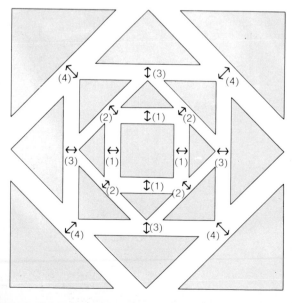

Continued on page 92

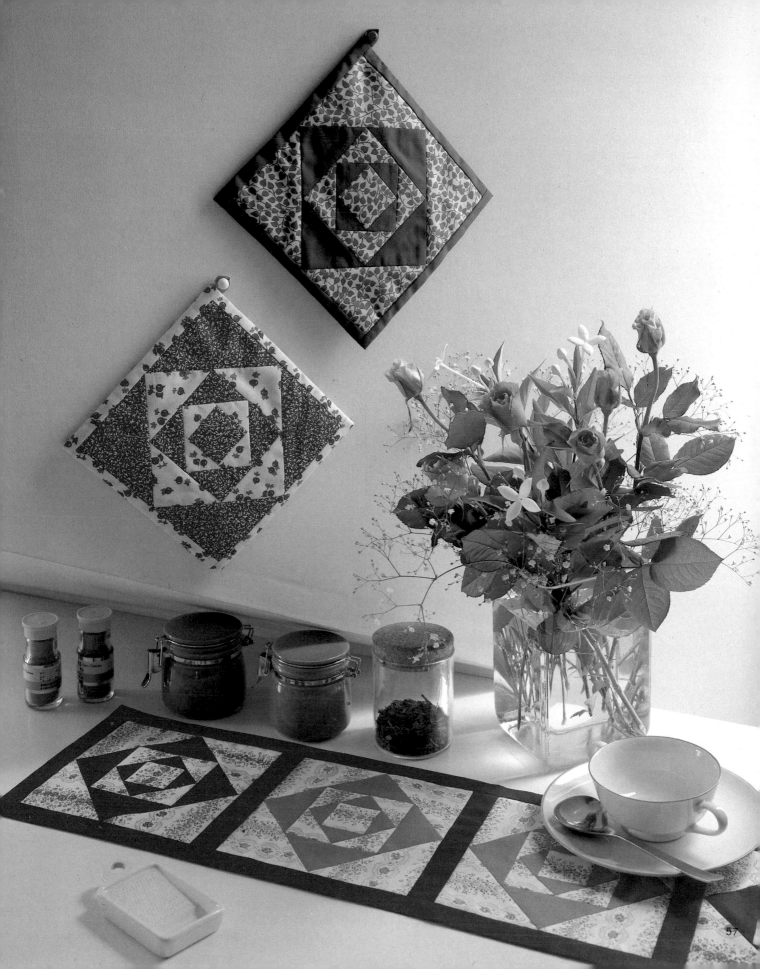

CHURN DASH
Wall Hanging and Bags

One of a number of similar patterns, such as Monkey Wrench and Hole in the Barn Door, this is an easy design, often worked in only two colors.

Wall Hanging (or Potholders)
for each square, you will need:
¼ yard of 45-inch wide print cotton (b)
  (includes lining and binding)
Scrap of print cotton (a)
  (or ⅛ yard if purchased)
¼ yard of fleece type batting
  (used double in potholders)
One button
Matching cotton thread
Finished size: 7⅜ inches × 7⅜ inches

Bags
For each bag, you will need:
¾ yard of 36- or 45-inch wide canvas or denim
Scraps of solid color and print cottons (a), (b), (c), and (d) (or ⅛ yard of each if purchased)
⅝ yard of 45-inch wide dressweight cotton lining
  (can be one of the above)
Scrap of lightweight backing
Scrap or ¼ yard of fleece type batting
Matching cotton thread
Finished size: 19 inches × 14 inches

Patterns of the patches used (actual size)
Add ¼-inch seam allowance

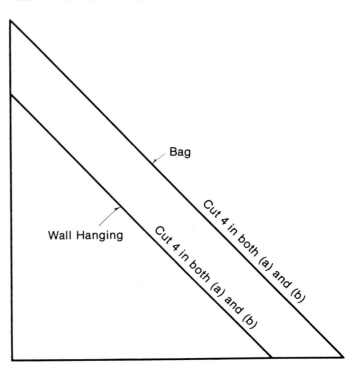

Bag
Cut 4 in both (a) and (b)

Wall Hanging
Cut 4 in both (a) and (b)

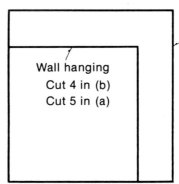

Bag Cut 4 in (d)
Cut 5 in (c)

Wall hanging
Cut 4 in (b)
Cut 5 in (a)

To make up
Join in sequences (1)–(4)

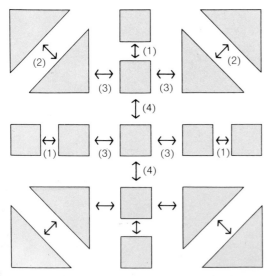

Continued on page 94

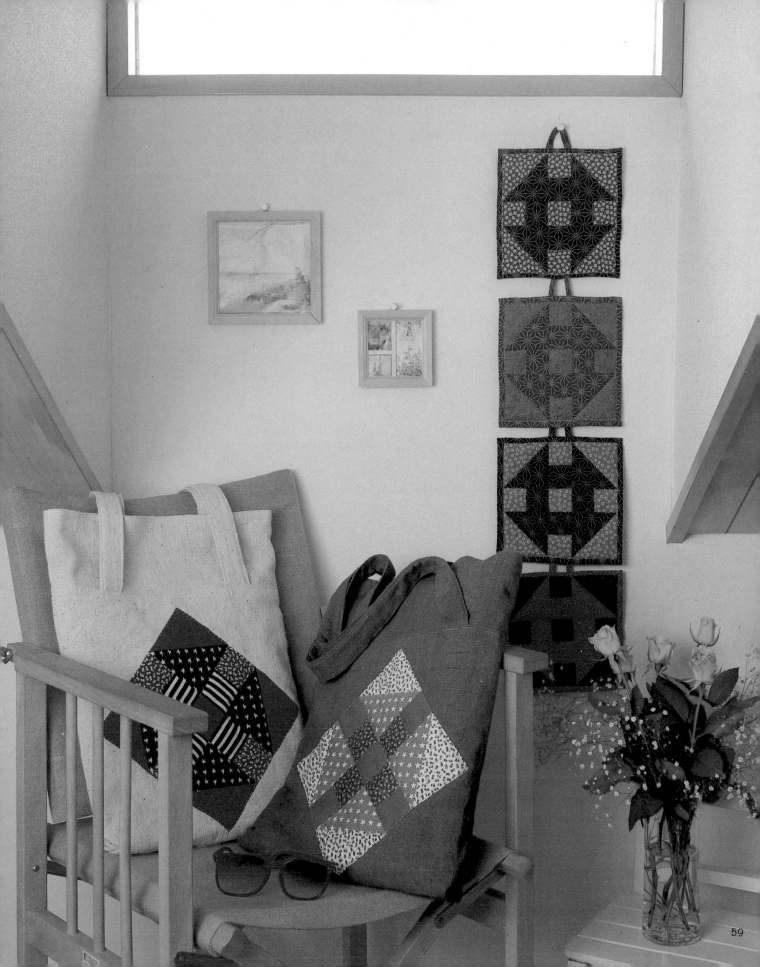

PINE TREE VARIATION
Pen Cases and Phone Set

**Multicolored abstract Pine Trees grow
endlessly up the length of pieced areas.**

Phone Set
For the phone cover, you will need:
½ yard of 45-inch wide yellow dressweight cotton
   (includes lining and border)
⅛ yard of 45-inch wide print cottons (a), (b), (c), and (d)
White cotton thread
Finished size: 13 inches × 14½ inches

For the mat, you will need:
⅜ yard of 45-inch wide yellow dressweight cotton
   (includes backing and binding)
⅛ yard of 45-inch wide print cottons (a) and (b)
Scrap of print cottons (c) and (d)
   (or ⅛ yard if purchased)
⅜ yard of fleece type batting
White cotton thread
Finished size: 10 inches × 9¼ inches

Pen Case
For each pen case, you will need:
⅜ yard of 45-inch wide solid color dressweight cotton (a)
   (includes binding and some patches)
⅛ yard of 45-inch wide print cotton (b)
   (includes backing and some patches)
Scrap or ⅛ yard of fleece type batting
½ inch of narrow Velcro™
White cotton thread
Finished size: 4¼ inches × 7½ inches (closed)

Patterns of the patches used (actual size)
Add ¼-inch seam allowance

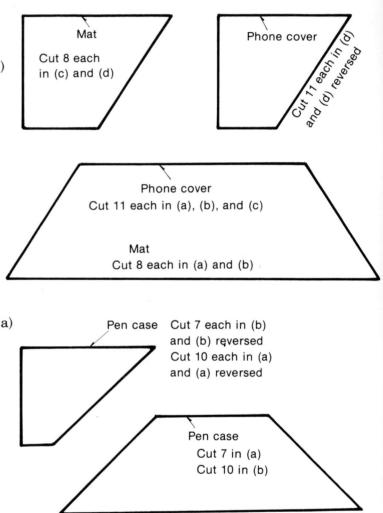

Mat
Cut 8 each in (c) and (d)

Phone cover
Cut 11 each in (d) and (d) reversed

Phone cover
Cut 11 each in (a), (b), and (c)

Mat
Cut 8 each in (a) and (b)

Pen case
Cut 7 each in (b) and (b) reversed
Cut 10 each in (a) and (a) reversed

Pen case
Cut 7 in (a)
Cut 10 in (b)

To make up
Join in sequences (1)–(2)
Press seam (1) open
Press seam (2) to one side for quilting

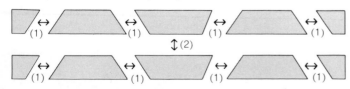

Continued on page 97

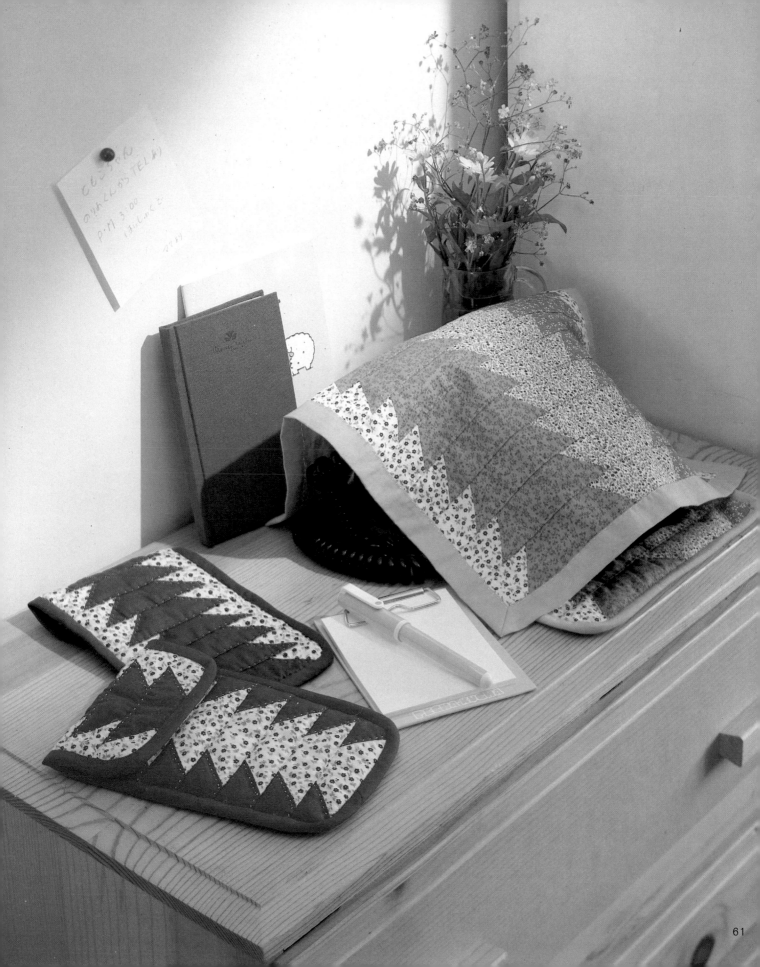

ODDFELLOW'S CROSS
Cushion and Bags

One of many Goose Chase designs, the cross is especially suitable to two-color planning.

Cushion
You will need:
1 yard of 45-inch wide olive green cotton
⅜ yard of 45-inch wide brown cotton
⅛ yard of 45-inch wide red print cotton
¾ yard of fleece type batting
¾ yard of lightweight backing
20-inch square inner cushion
Olive green and brown cotton thread
Finished size: 19⅝ inches × 19⅝ inches

Bags
For the navy bag (bottom right), you will need:
⅝ yard of 36- or 45-inch wide navy canvas
Scraps of solid white and solid navy dressweight
    cotton (or ⅛ yard of each if purchased)
½ yard of 45-inch wide dressweight lining
¼ yard of fleece type batting
¼ yard of lightweight backing
Navy cotton thread
Finished size: 18 inches × 16 inches

For the white bag (top right), you will need:
⅝ yard of 36- or 45-inch wide white canvas
Scraps of solid red and plaid dressweight cotton
    (or ⅛ yard of each if purchased)
⅜ yard of 45-inch wide pale blue dressweight cotton
    (includes pocket lining and some patches)
½ yard of 45-inch wide dressweight lining
Matching cotton thread
Finished size: 18 inches × 16 inches

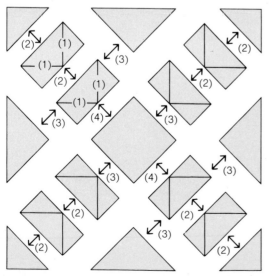

To make up
Join in sequences (1)–(4)

Add ¼-inch seam allowance

Total number for each project.

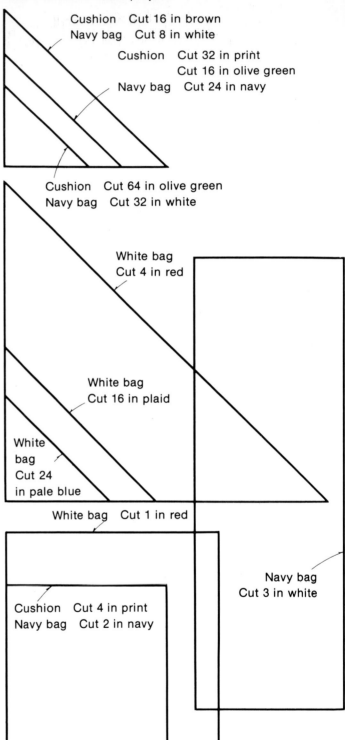

Cushion   Cut 16 in brown
Navy bag   Cut 8 in white

Cushion   Cut 32 in print
            Cut 16 in olive green
Navy bag   Cut 24 in navy

Cushion   Cut 64 in olive green
Navy bag   Cut 32 in white

White bag
Cut 4 in red

White bag
Cut 16 in plaid

White
bag
Cut 24
in pale blue

White bag   Cut 1 in red

Navy bag
Cut 3 in white

Cushion   Cut 4 in print
Navy bag   Cut 2 in navy

Continued on page 99

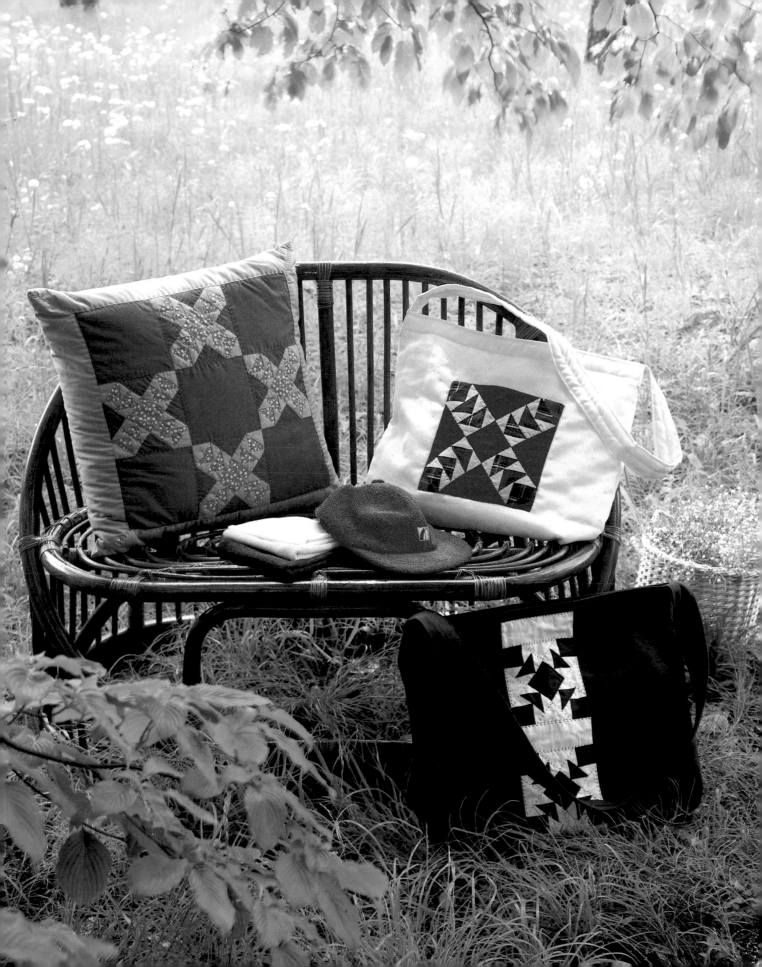

CRIB OR LAP QUILT

As shown on page 1

To make up:

(1) Cut out patch pieces, adding ¼-inch seam allowance. Join as shown on the chart.

(2) Place the batting between the pieced top and the backing. Baste it in place, starting at the center and working outward. Quilt entire piece, then finish the edges with binding.

Chart of Measurements

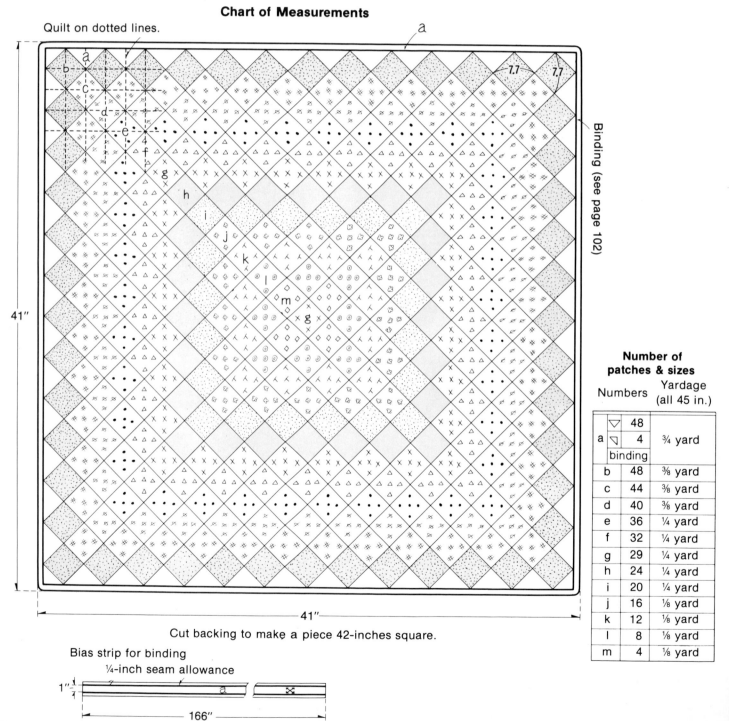

Quilt on dotted lines.

41"

41"

Cut backing to make a piece 42-inches square.

Bias strip for binding

¼-inch seam allowance

1"

166"

Binding (see page 102)

Number of patches & sizes

		Numbers	Yardage (all 45 in.)
a	▽	48	¾ yard
a	◁	4	
	binding		
b		48	⅜ yard
c		44	⅜ yard
d		40	⅜ yard
e		36	¼ yard
f		32	¼ yard
g		29	¼ yard
h		24	¼ yard
i		20	¼ yard
j		16	⅛ yard
k		12	⅛ yard
l		8	⅛ yard
m		4	⅛ yard

YOUTH BED QUILT
As shown on page 5

To make up:
(1) Cut out patch pieces adding ¼-inch seam allowance and join as shown on page 2. Alternate blocks A and B as shown below.

(2) Join border strips to top piece crosswise and then lengthwise. Place batting between top piece and backing, quilt and finish the edges with binding.

Chart of Measurements

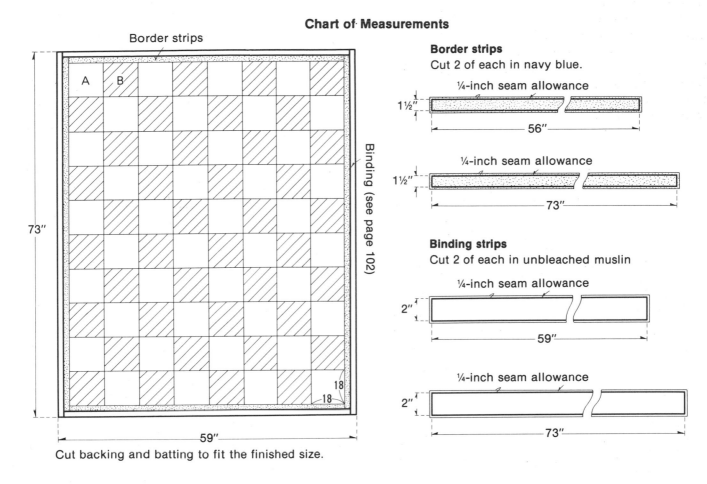

Border strips

A B

73"

Binding (see page 102)

18
18

59"

Cut backing and batting to fit the finished size.

Border strips
Cut 2 of each in navy blue.

¼-inch seam allowance
1½"
56"

¼-inch seam allowance
1½"
73"

Binding strips
Cut 2 of each in unbleached muslin

¼-inch seam allowance
2"
59"

¼-inch seam allowance
2"
73"

The quilt is composed of 40 pieced blocks and 40 pieced and quilted blocks.

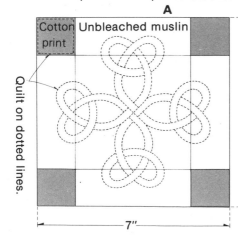

A

Cotton print   Unbleached muslin

Quilt on dotted lines.

7"

7"

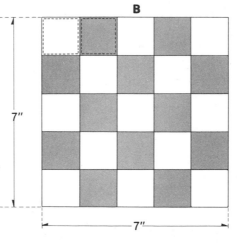

B

7"

7"

To finish corner of binding

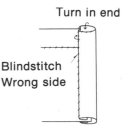

Turn in end

Blindstitch
Wrong side

Each block requires 12 pieces (total) of cotton print and plain cotton selected at random and 13 pieces of unbleached muslin.

CRIB OR LAP QUILT
As shown on page 3

To make up:
(1) Cut out patch pieces, adding ¼-inch seam allowance. Join as shown on the chart.
(2) Join border strips to pieced top crosswise then lengthwise. Place batting between top piece and backing. Baste all three together, working from the center outward. Quilt and finish the edges with binding.

Chart of Measurements

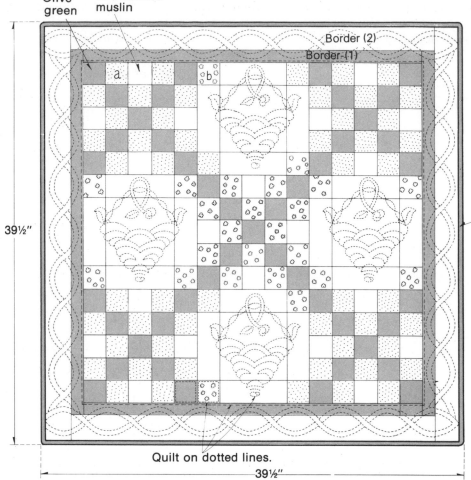

Olive green

Unbleached muslin

Border (2)
Border (1)

39½"

Binding (see page 102)

Quilt on dotted lines.

39½"

Cut olive green backing to make a piece 40-inches square.

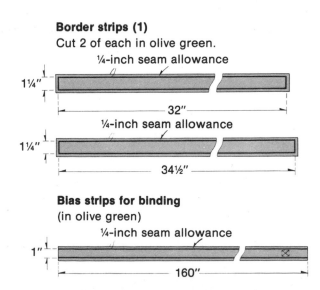

Border strips (1)
Cut 2 of each in olive green.
¼-inch seam allowance
1¼"
32"
¼-inch seam allowance
1¼"
34½"

Bias strips for binding
(in olive green)
¼-inch seam allowance
1"
160"

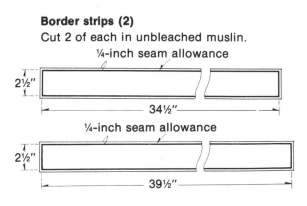

Border strips (2)
Cut 2 of each in unbleached muslin.
¼-inch seam allowance
2½"
34½"
¼-inch seam allowance
2½"
39½"

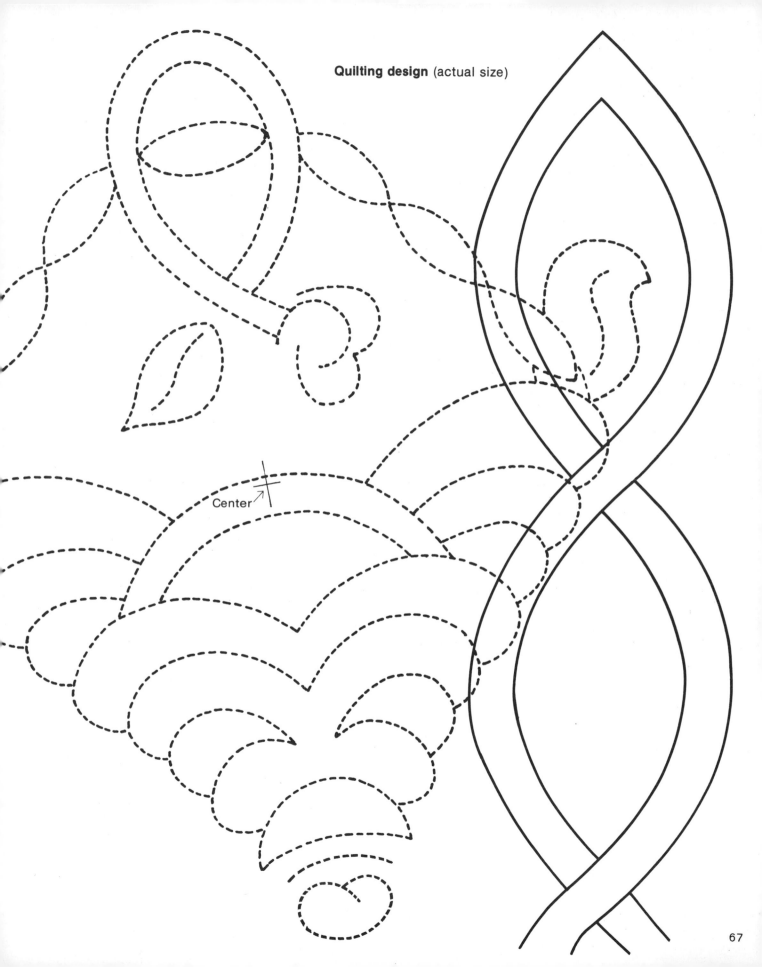

Quilting design (actual size)

Center

LAP QUILT OR THROW
As shown on page 7

To make up:

(1) Cut out patch pieces, adding ¼-inch seam allowance. Cut squares in backing and batting. With right sides together, stitch patch pieces to backing and batting, as shown.

(2) With right sides together, seam top pieces of blocks. Overlap batting edges and blindstitch backing in place.

(3) Finish the edges with binding.

Chart of Measurements

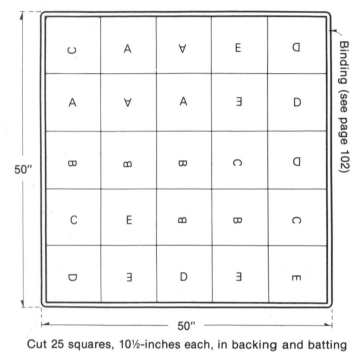

50″ (left side)

50″ (bottom)

Binding (see page 102) (right side)

Cut 25 squares, 10½-inches each, in backing and batting

Colors

Use four shades of each except red. Yardages are given for 45-inch fabrics, or scraps can be used.

Colors		Yardage (all 45 in.)	Colors		Yardage (all 45 in.)
Lilac	a	⅛ yard	Yellow	a	⅛ yard
	b	⅛ yard		b	⅛ yard
	c	¼ yard		c	¼ yard
	d	¼ yard		d	¼ yard
Brown	a	⅛ yard	Gray	a	⅛ yard
	b	⅛ yard		b	⅛ yard
	c	¼ yard		c	¼ yard
	d	¼ yard		d	¼ yard
Blue	a	⅛ yard	Green	a	⅛ yard
	b	⅛ yard		b	⅛ yard
	c	¼ yard		c	¼ yard
	d	¼ yard		d	¼ yard
Pink	a	⅛ yard	Orange	a	⅛ yard
	b	⅛ yard		b	⅛ yard
	c	¼ yard		c	⅛ yard
	d	¼ yard		d	⅛ yard
			Red		¼ yard

Color scheme of each block

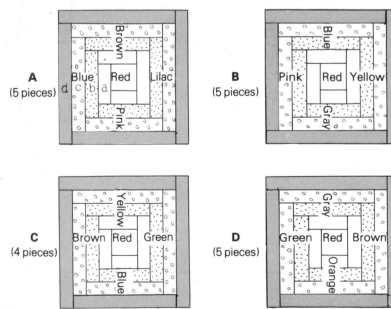

A (5 pieces)

B (5 pieces)

C (4 pieces)

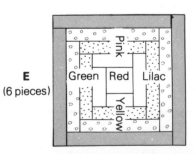

D (5 pieces)

E (6 pieces)

①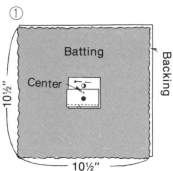

②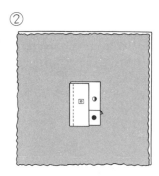

③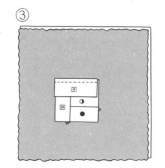

④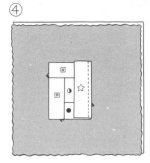

Batting

Backing

Center

10½"

10½"

Pin the center piece (◑) to the center of the foundation block. With right sides together, stitch piece marked (●).

⑤

⑥

Continue to seam top layers to form five strips of five blocks each.

⑦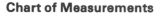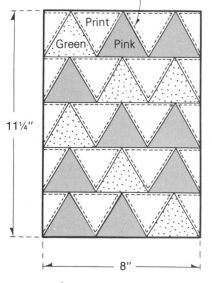

⑧

Backing

With right sides together, seam the top layers of two blocks.

Backing

Seam allowance

Overlap batting. Fold under ¼-inch on one edge of the backing and blind-stitch in place, always starting and ending ½ inch from the ends.
Join the strips together by repeating steps 7 and 8 on the long sides of the five strips.

BED LINEN AND MATCHING PICTURE

As shown on page 13

Patchwork Picture
To make up:
(1) Cut out patch pieces, adding ¼-inch seam allowance. Join as shown on page 12 and the chart.
(2) Place batting between pieced top and backing.
(3) Quilt as indicated.

Chart of Measurements
Quilt on dotted lines

Print
Green
Pink

11¼"

8"

Patchwork Border
To make up:
(1) Cut out and join the patch pieces as shown on page 12 and the chart.
(2) With right sides together, seam pieced top and backing together (with batting on wrong side of top if you plan to use it) and leave an opening for turning. Turn right side out and blindstitch the opening.
(3) Topstitch or quilt as indicated.

Chart of Measurements

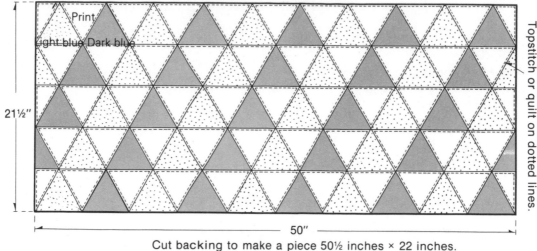

Cut backing to make a piece 50½ inches × 22 inches.
Continue to width of sheet if desired.

Pillowcase
To make up:
(1) Cut out and join patch pieces as shown on page 12 and the chart.
(2) With wrong sides together (including batting if you plan to use it), baste pieced top to backing.
(3) Topstitch or quilt as indicated.
(4) Hem the two edge of the pillowcase back pieces and overlap, as shown. With right sides together, seam pieced pillow front to overlapped pillow back.

Chart of Measurements

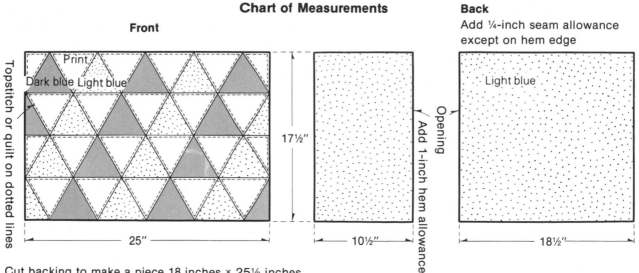

Front

Back
Add ¼-inch seam allowance except on hem edge

Light blue

Cut backing to make a piece 18 inches × 25½ inches

To overlap the two back pieces

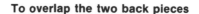

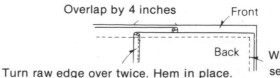

Overlap by 4 inches

Front

Back

Turn raw edge over twice. Hem in place.

With right sides together, seam front to back.

CRIB QUILT
As shown on page 9

To make up:
(1) Use the paper-liner method (see page 101). Cut enough paper linings to make up a large portion of the quilt at one time.
(2) Cut out patch pieces, adding ¼-inch seam allowance. Cut sets of 6 pentagon patches from each print, yellow small hexagons, navy blue large hexagons, and print and navy border pieces, as shown on page 8 and the chart.
(3) Place batting between the pieced top and the backing. Quilt along the seamlines. Finish the edges with binding.

Chart of Measurements

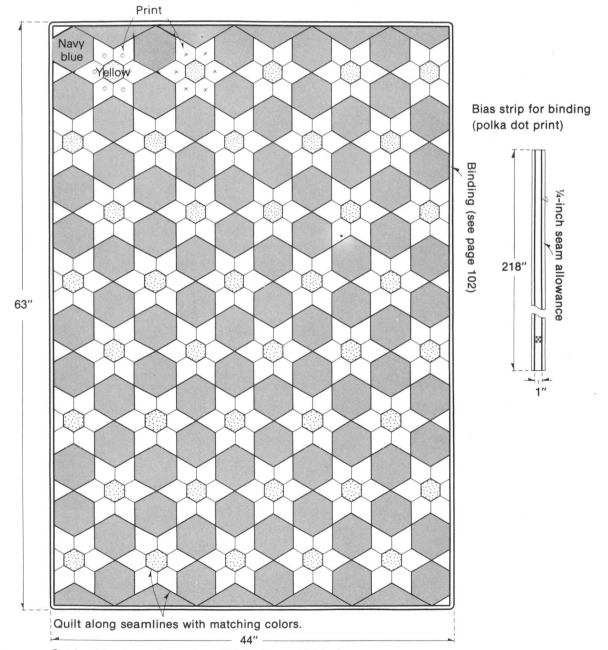

Print

Navy blue

Yellow

63″

44″

Binding (see page 102)

Bias strip for binding (polka dot print)

218″

¼-inch seam allowance

1″

Quilt along seamlines with matching colors.

Cut backing to make a piece 63½ inches × 44½ inches.

TABLECLOTH
As shown on page 11

To make up:
(1) Cut out patch pieces, adding ¼-inch seam allowance.
Cut 10 pieces in royal blue cotton for the background,
as shown on the chart and listed in the cutting guide,
adding ¼-inch seam allowance all around.
(2) Join patch pieces, as shown on page 10 and the chart.
(3) With top piece and lining right sides together, seam
all around, leaving only about 10 inches open for turning.
Turn right side out. Blindstitch the opening to finish.

Chart of Measurements

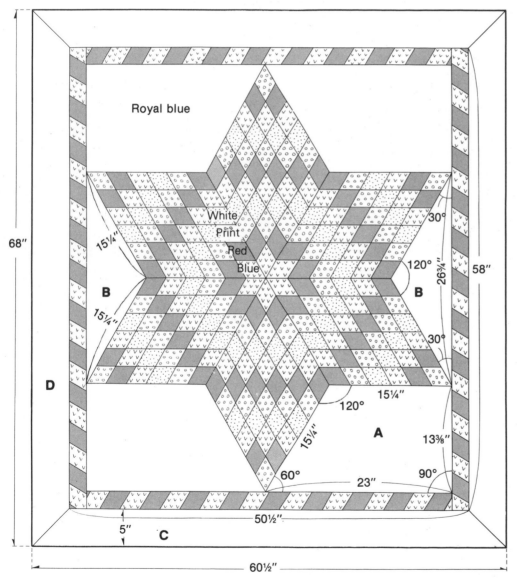

Royal blue

White
Print
Red
Blue

68"

15¼"

B

15¼"

D

30°

120°

26¾"

58"

30°

15¼"

120°

A

13⅜"

15¼"

60°

23"

90°

50½"

5"

C

60½"

Cutting guide
Cut 2 royal blue A
Cut 2 royal blue A reversed
Cut 2 royal blue B
Cut 2 royal blue C
Cut 2 royal blue D

Cut and seam lining to make a piece 61 inches × 68½ inches.
Add ¼-inch seam allowance to all pieces.

PLACEMATS AND PINCUSHIONS
As shown on page 15

Placemat
To make up:
(1) Cut out patch pieces, adding ¼-inch seam allowance. Join as shown on page 14 and the chart.
(2) Place batting and backing on the wrong side of the pieced top. Quilt and finish the edges with bias binding.

Chart of Measurements

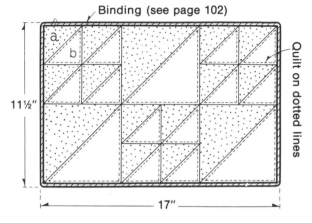

Pincushions
To make up:
(1) Cut out and join patch pieces as shown in the chart.
(2) With right sides together, seam front to back, leaving an opening for turning. Turn right side out and stuff firmly with filler. Blindstitch opening to finish.

Chart of Measurements

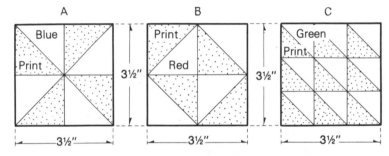

Cut 4-inch squares in blue, red, and green for the back of pincushions A, B, and C, respectively.

BED LINEN AND TRAY CLOTH
As shown on page 19

Tray Cloth
To make up:
(1) Cut out patch pieces, adding ¼-inch seam allowance. Join as shown on page 18 and the chart.
(2) Place batting between the pieced top and the backing.
(3) Quilt along seamlines.

Chart of Measurements

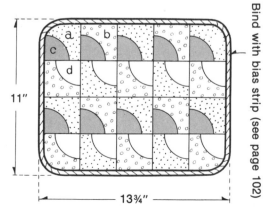

Patchwork Border
To make up:
(1) Assemble patches as shown on page 18 and the chart.
(2) With right sides of lace and backing to right side of pieced top, seam the edges, curving and trimming corners, leaving an opening for turning. (Include batting on wrong side of top if you plan to use it.) Turn right side out. Blindstitch the opening to finish.
(3) Topstitch or quilt as indicated.

Chart of Measurements

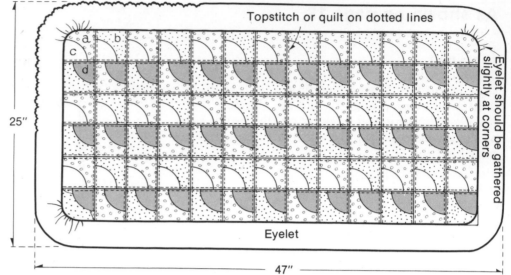

Topstitch or quilt on dotted lines

Eyelet should be gathered slightly at corners

Eyelet

25″

47″

Cut backing (and batting) 41½ inches × 19½ inches

Pillowcase
To make up:
(1) Assemble patches as shown on page 18 and the chart
(2) Lay backing (and batting, if used) on wrong side of pieced top and topstitch or quilt as indicated.

(3) Hem the raw edges of pillowcase back piece and overlap, as shown. With right sides together and eyelet between, seam pieced pillow front to overlapped pillow back, curving and trimming corners.

Chart of Measurements

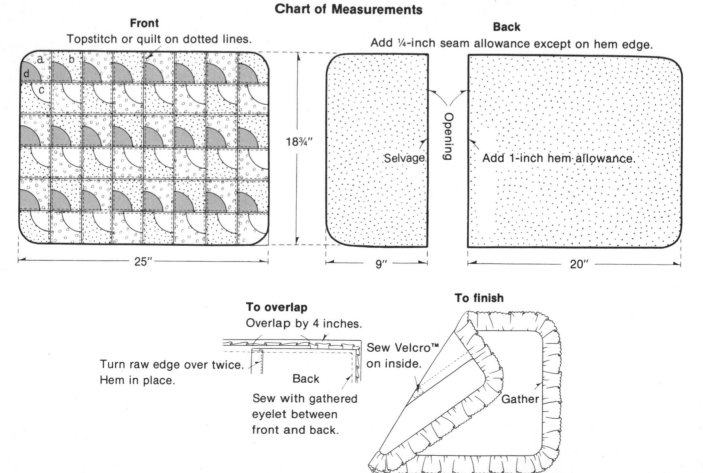

Front
Topstitch or quilt on dotted lines.

25″

18¾″

Back
Add ¼-inch seam allowance except on hem edge.

Opening

Selvage

Add 1-inch hem allowance.

9″

20″

To overlap
Overlap by 4 inches.

Turn raw edge over twice. Hem in place.

Back

Sew with gathered eyelet between front and back.

To finish

Sew Velcro™ on inside.

Gather

74

TABLECLOTH

As shown on page 17

To make up:
(1) Cut out patch pieces, adding ¼-inch seam allowance. Join as shown on page 16 and in the chart, positioning the 12 brown pieces, as described on page 16, around the edge.
(2) Cut the lining to size, leaving a generous allowance outside the dimensions of the pieced top. Baste the two pieces right sides together.
(3) Seam around the edge of the large hexagon, following the design of the pieced top and leaving an opening for turning. Turn right side out. Blindstitch the opening to finish. Lay the entire piece on a flat surface and pin at intervals.
(4) Turn under the seam allowance around the print patches and baste in place. Topstitch onto the lining, as shown on the chart, so that the lining forms the central patches.

Chart of Measurements

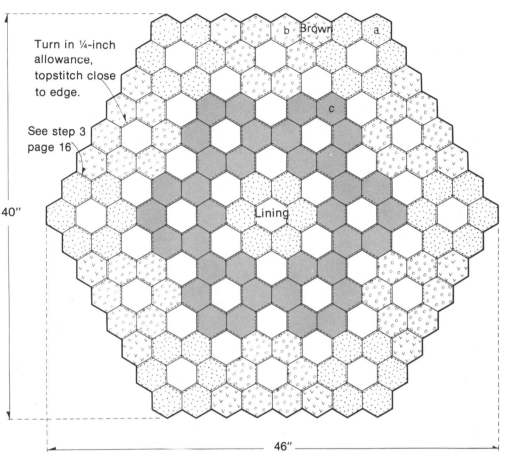

Cut the lining to fit the pieced top, adding a generous allowance at each edge. Excess can be trimmed after seaming.

CUSHIONS

As shown on page 35

To make up:
(1) Cut out patch pieces, adding ¼-inch seam allowance. Join patches to make flowers, as shown.
(2) Blindstitch flower, stem, and leaves to pillow front.
(3) Seam front and back right sides together, leaving opening for turning.
(4) Stuff with synthetic filler and blindstitch opening to finish.

Chart of Measurements

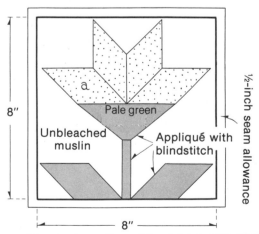

Cut front from unbleached muslin and back from pale green.

PANEL

As shown on page 21

To make up:

(1) Cut out patch pieces, adding ¼-inch seam allowance. Join as shown on page 21 and the chart.

(2) Place pieced top and backing wrong sides together (with batting between, if you plan to use it) and round off corners.

(3) If batting is used, quilt along seamlines before binding. Bind edges together with narrow bias binding (see page 102).

Chart of Measurements

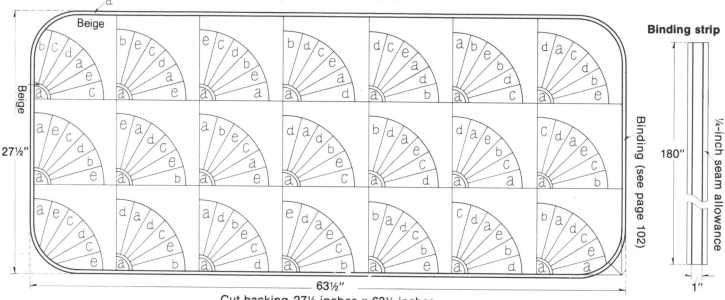

27½"

63½"

Cut backing 27½ inches × 63½ inches

Binding strip

180"

¼-inch seam allowance

Binding (see page 102)

1"

WALL HANGING AND PHONE SET

As shown on page 21

Phone cover
To make up:

(1) Cut out patch pieces, adding ¼-inch seam allowance. Join as shown on page 21 and the chart.

(2) Join the blocks with center strips. Place pieced top and backing wrong sides together and finish the edges with binding.

(3) Topstitch center strips and bindings, as shown on chart.

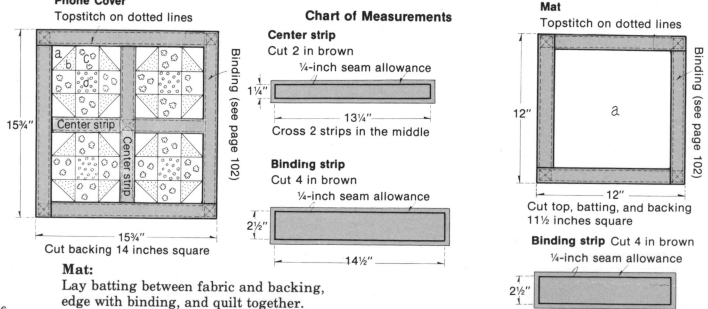

Phone Cover
Topstitch on dotted lines

15¾"

15¾"

Binding (see page 102)

Center strip

Cut backing 14 inches square

Mat:
Lay batting between fabric and backing, edge with binding, and quilt together.

Chart of Measurements

Center strip
Cut 2 in brown
¼-inch seam allowance

1¼"

13¼"

Cross 2 strips in the middle

Binding strip
Cut 4 in brown
¼-inch seam allowance

2½"

14½"

Mat
Topstitch on dotted lines

12"

12"

Binding (see page 102)

a

Cut top, batting, and backing
11½ inches square

Binding strip Cut 4 in brown
¼-inch seam allowance

2½"

11"

Wall Hanging
To make up:

(1) Cut out patch pieces. Join as shown on page 21 and the chart.
(2) Place batting between pieced top and backing. Quilt as indicated. Finish edges with binding.
(3) Place batting between foundation fabric and backing. Sew pockets in position, and quilt foundation as shown on the chart.
(4) Finish the edges with binding. Sew loops to the top.

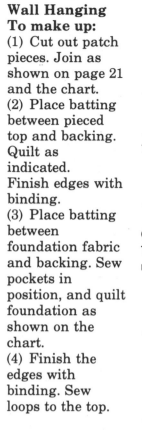

Pocket (make 2)
Quilt on dotted lines

7⅜"

7⅜"

Cut backing and batting 7⅜ inches square, round off corners.

Binding strip (cut 2 in (d))
¼-inch seam allowance

1"

30"

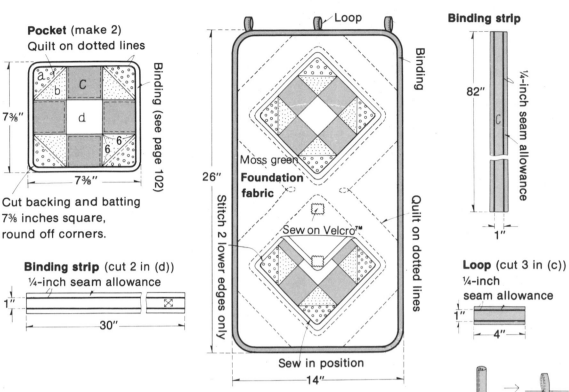

Loop

Binding

Moss green
Foundation fabric

Sew on Velcro™

26"

Stitch 2 lower edges only

Quilt on dotted lines

Sew in position

14"

Cut a piece 26 inches × 14 inches in moss green foundation fabric, backing, and batting. Round corners.

Binding strip

82"

¼-inch seam allowance

C

1"

Loop (cut 3 in (c))
¼-inch seam allowance

1"

4"

Topstitch   Sew on

TABLE MAT AND POTHOLDERS
As shown on page 23

Table Mat
To make up:

(1) Cut out patch pieces, adding ¼-inch seam allowance. Join as shown on page 22 and the chart.
(2) Place batting between pieced top and backing. Quilt as indicated.
(3) Finish edges with binding. Topstitch, as shown.

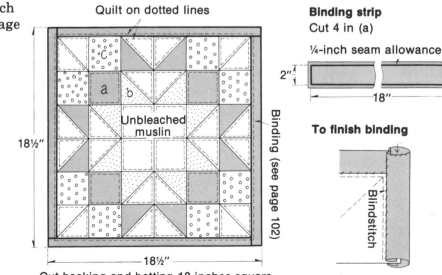

Chart of Measurements

Quilt on dotted lines

c

a   b

Unbleached muslin

Binding (see page 102)

18½"

18½"

Cut backing and batting 18 inches square.

Binding strip
Cut 4 in (a)

¼-inch seam allowance

2"

18"

To finish binding

Blindstitch

Potholder

To make up:

(1) Cut out patch pieces, adding ¼-inch seam allowance. Join as shown on page 22 and the chart.

(2) Place double batting between pieced top and backing. Quilt as indicated.

(3) Finish edges with binding. Sew on loop.

Chart of Measurements

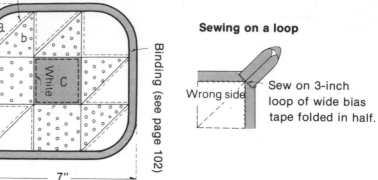

Quilt on dotted lines.

Binding (see page 102)

7"

7"

White c

a b

Cut backing 7 inches square.
Cut batting 7 inches square, double thickness.
Round corners as shown.

Sewing on a loop

Wrong side

Sew on 3-inch loop of wide bias tape folded in half.

BAG AND PEN CASE

As shown on page 25

Bag

To make up:

Cut out patch pieces, adding ¼-inch seam allowance. Join as shown on page 24 and the chart.

(2) Place batting and backing on wrong side of pieced pocket. Quilt together. Bind edges.

(3) Cut out each piece as shown. Bind upper edge of front and edges of strap. Sew pocket to flap.

(4) Lay front and back wrong sides together and stitch close to raw edges. Bind the edges. Make up and sew on straps and ties.

Chart of measurements

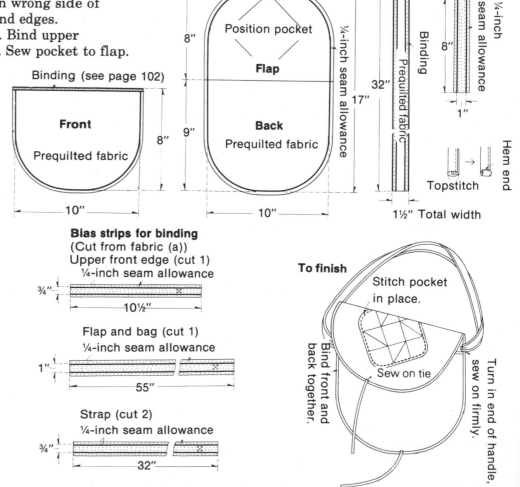

Position pocket

Flap

8"

Front
Prequilted fabric

Binding (see page 102)

8"

10"

9"

Back
Prequilted fabric

¼-inch seam allowance

17"

10"

Strap

32"

Binding

Prequilted fabric

Tie
(cut 2 in (a))

8"

1"

¼-inch seam allowance

Hem end

Topstitch

1½" Total width

Bias strips for binding
(Cut from fabric (a))
Upper front edge (cut 1)
¼-inch seam allowance

¾"

10½"

Flap and bag (cut 1)
¼-inch seam allowance

1"

55"

Strap (cut 2)
¼-inch seam allowance

¾"

32"

To finish

Stitch pocket in place.

Sew on tie

Bind front and back together.

Turn in end of handle, sew on firmly.

Pocket
Quilt on dotted lines

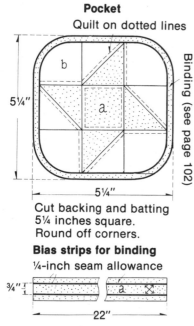

b

a

5¼"

5¼"

Binding (see page 102)

Cut backing and batting 5¼ inches square.
Round off corners.

Bias strips for binding
¼-inch seam allowance

¾"

a

22"

78

Pen Case
To make up:

(1) Cut out patch pieces adding ¼-inch seam allowance. Join as for the bag.
(2) Cut one piece, 2 inches × 3 inches, and one piece, 1½ inches × 3 inches, adding ¼-inch seam allowance, from (b).
(3) Join pieced square to two (b) pieces and round lower corners, as shown on the chart.
(4) Place batting and backing on the wrong side of front piece and quilt as indicated. Layer back piece in same way.
(5) Bind top edge of front.
(6) Lay front and back pieces together, as shown on the chart, stitch near the edge. Bind around.
(7) Sew on snap.

Chart of Measurements

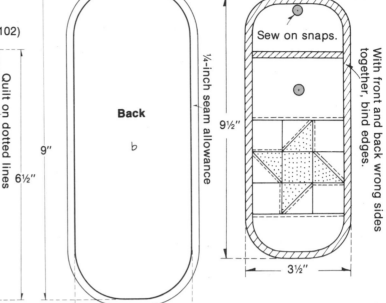

Binding (see page 102)

Front

b

b

a

2"

¼-inch seam allowance

Quilt on dotted lines

9"

6½"

b 1½"

3"

Back

b

¼-inch seam allowance

3"

Cut backing and batting to the size of back and front pieces.

To finish

Sew on snaps.

With front and back wrong sides together, bind edges.

¼-inch seam allowance

9½"

3½"

VANITY BAG AND EYEGLASS CASE
As shown on page 25

Vanity Bag
To make up:

(1) Cut out patch pieces, adding ¼-inch seam allowance. Join as shown on page 24 and the chart, making two pieced squares.
(2) Cut two strips, 1¼ inches × 9½ inches, adding ¼-inch seam allowance, from (b).
(3) Join the two pieced squares to the two (b) strips, as shown on the chart.
(4) Place batting between assembled piece and backing. Quilt as indicated.
(5) Bind both ends.

Chart of Measurements

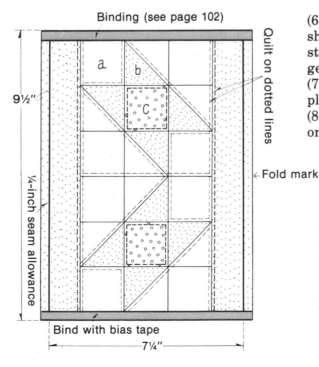

Binding (see page 102)

a   b

c

9½"

¼-inch seam allowance

Quilt on dotted lines

← Fold mark

Bind with bias tape

7¼"

(6) Fold the piece across, as shown in the chart, and stitch the folded ends together close to the edge.
(7) Handstitch zipper in place.
(8) Bind the ends, as shown on the chart.

To finish

Stitch zipper to binding.

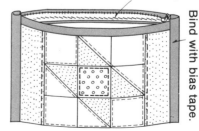

Bind with bias tape.

Eyeglass Case

To make up:

(1) Cut out the patch pieces, adding ¼-inch seam allowance. Join as for the vanity case.

(2) Cut two pieces, 1½ inches × 4⅛ inches, adding ¼-inch seam allowance, from (a).

(3) Join the pieced square to the two (a) pieces, as shown on the chart.

(4) Place batting and backing on the wrong side of front pieces and quilt as indicated. Layer back piece, batting, and backing and baste together around the edges.

(5) Bind upper edges of both front and back piece to end of opening, as shown on the chart.

(6) Lay front and back together, as shown on the chart, and stitch close to the raw edges. Bind around, turning under ends and hand finishing over the upper binding.

Chart of Measurements

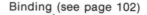

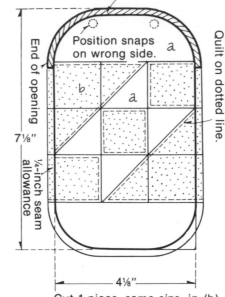

Binding (see page 102)

Position snaps on wrong side.

End of opening

Quilt on dotted line.

¼-inch seam allowance

7⅛"

4⅛"

Cut 1 piece, same size, in (b) for back piece, 2 pieces in (a) for backing, and 2 pieces of batting. Round off all corners.

To finish

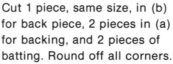

End of opening

Sew on snaps

End of opening

With front and back wrong sides together, bind edges as far as end of opening.

7⅝"

4⅝"

CRIB QUILT
As shown on page 27

To make up:

(1) Cut out patch pieces for the top and backing. Sew as shown on page 26. Join, referring to the chart. Stuff.

(2) In seaming the pieces together, refer to the chart for color arrangement.

(3) Pin or baste the pieced top to the lining, with wrong sides together. Bind edges crosswise, then lengthwise, stuffing gently as you hem down the back edge by hand.

Chart of Measurements

Front

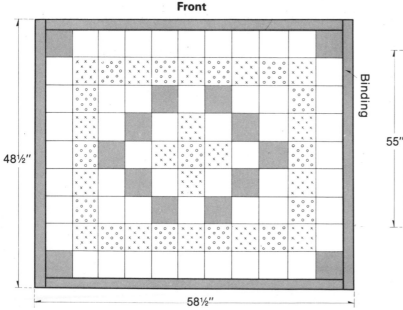

Binding

48½"

58½"

Cut the lining in gray-green cotton to make a piece 55 inches × 45 inches.

Binding strips
(cut 2 of each)

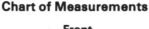

55"

48½"

¼-inch seam allowance

3½"

3½"

Color scheme and number of patches

Color	Number
Pink	52
Pink print	18
Pink-and-white	15
Gray-green	14

To finish binding

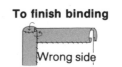

Wrong side

Stuff binding gently, as you stitch it to the back (see page 102).

CUSHION AND PINCUSHIONS

As shown on page 31

Cushion
To make up:
(1) Cut out patch pieces in appropriate fabrics. Join as shown on page 30.
(2) Cut out 2 pieces, as shown, for pillow back.
(3) Stitch zipper between back pieces.
(4) Lay pieced top and back right sides together (with zipper partly open for turning) and seam edges. Take a scant ⅛-inch seam on pieced top, ¼-inch seam on pillow back.
(5) Slip inner cushion through zipper opening.

Pincushions
To make up:
(1) Cut out patches. Join as shown on page 30.
(2) With right sides together, seam pieced top to pincushion back of solid color fabric. Take scant ⅛-inch seam on pieced top, ½-inch seam on solid color back. Leave small opening for turning.
(3) Turn right side out and stuff firmly with synthetic filler.
(4) For pink pincushion insert corded piping in edge. (See corded piping instructions for toaster cover on page 84.)

Chart of Measurements

Front — Muslin — Print ⅛-inch seam allowance — 18¾" — Omit decorative patches at edge — 18¾"

Back — Muslin — Sew in zipper — ¼-inch seam allowance — 9½" — 9½" — ½-inch seam allowance

Chart of Measurements

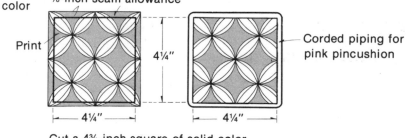

Solid color — Print — ⅛-inch seam allowance — 4¼" — 4¼" — Corded piping for pink pincushion — 4¼"

Cut a 4¾-inch square of solid color for pincushion back.

PINCUSHION

As shown on page 49

To make up:
(1) Cut out patch pieces, adding ¼-inch seam allowance Join four pieces together, as shown on page 48.
(2) Cut back and front pieces, 4¼-inches square with ½-inch seam allowance added all around.
(3) Appliqué pieces to center of front piece. Place batting only on wrong side of top piece and quilt as indicated.
(4) Seam front and back right sides together, leaving 2½-inch opening on one side for turning.
(5) Turn right side out, stuff, and blindstitch opening to finish.

Cut 2 pieces of foundation fabric and 1 piece of batting 5¼-inches square

Chart of Measurements

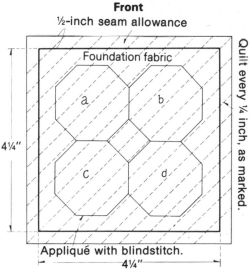

Front — ½-inch seam allowance — Foundation fabric — Quilt every ¼ inch, as marked. — a — b — c — d — 4¼" — Appliqué with blindstitch. — 4¼"

CRIB OR LAP QUILT

As shown on page 29

To make up:

(1) Cut out patch pieces, adding ¼-inch seam allowance. Join patches to make up pieces A and B, then arrange and join, as shown on page 28 and the chart.

(2) Cut batting to size and baste on wrong side of pieced top. Seam pieced top and backing right sides together, following shape of top edge. Leave opening for turning. Trim seams, clipping into Vs.

(3) Turn piece right side out. Quilt as indicated, shaping edges first.

Chart of Measurements

Quilt on dotted lines

35"

43"

Cut backing in fabric (a), 44 inches × 36 inches

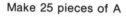
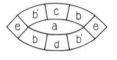
Make 25 pieces of A

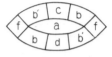
Make 24 pieces of B

BAG

As shown on page 33

To make up:

(1) Cut out patch and appliqué pieces, adding ¼-inch seam allowance. Join as shown on page 32 and the chart.

(2) Cut main piece 25 inches × 13 inches (including hem and seams) from the prequilted cotton.

(3) Position the motif, as shown, and topstitch to the main piece.

(4) Finish the edges of the pocket with binding. Position the pocket, as shown, and topstitch to the main piece.

(5) Attach handles, and hem top edge as shown.

(6) With right sides together, seam sides. Miter lower corners 2 inches across to form base, as shown.

Chart of Measurements

1½-inch hem allowance

Prequilted fabric   2"

Secure with topstitch

Pocket

22"

Fold

12"

½-inch seam allowance

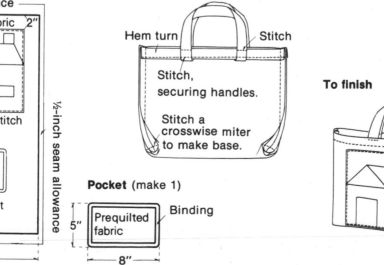

Hem turn   Stitch

Stitch, securing handles.

Stitch a crosswise miter to make base.

To finish

Pocket (make 1)

Prequilted fabric   Binding

5"

8"

TWIN-BED QUILT
As shown on page 45

To make up:
(1) Cut out patch pieces, adding ¼-inch seam allowance. Assemble, alternating light and dark colors, as shown.
(2) Lay batting between pieced top and backing. Quilt as indicated.
(3) Bind edges.

Chart of Measurements

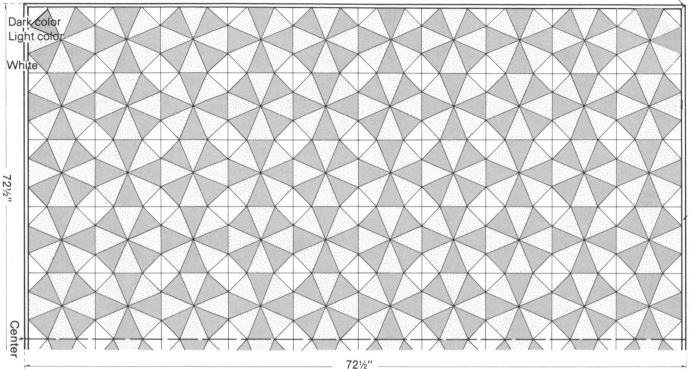

Dark color
Light color
White
Miter corner
Binding (see page 102)
72½"
Center
72½"

Seam and cut backing to make a piece 73 inches square.

Bias binding strip (Cream)
¼-inch seam allowance

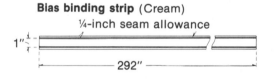

1"
292"

TOASTER COVER, TEA COZY, AND CUSHIONS
As shown on page 37

Toaster Cover
To make up:
(1) Scale up design (see page 36). Cut out pieces, adding ¼-inch seam allowance.
(2) Cut front, back, and center panel from lime green, as shown on page 84, adding ½-inch seam allowance. Appliqué figures to front with blindstitch, inserting braid between hat and foundation fabric on girl. Finish with embroidery (see page 84).
(3) Pin or baste batting and backing to wrong side of all three pieces of cover. Stitch piping on right side of the curved edge of front and back piece, along the seamline, so that raw edges of piping and

of fabric are in the same direction. (Use machine zipper or cording foot.)
(4) Following the stitching line for cording, seam the center panel right sides together with the two side pieces.
(5) If bias tape is used on bottom edge, lay piping between it and lower edge of cozy and seam all around. Turn bias up into cozy and hem in place over raw edge of piping, as shown on page 84.
(6) If lining is used, cut and make it up to fit inside the cozy. Stitch piping to lower edge of outer piece. Turn lower edge of lining under ½ inch and blindstitch it to cover raw edges of cozy and piping.

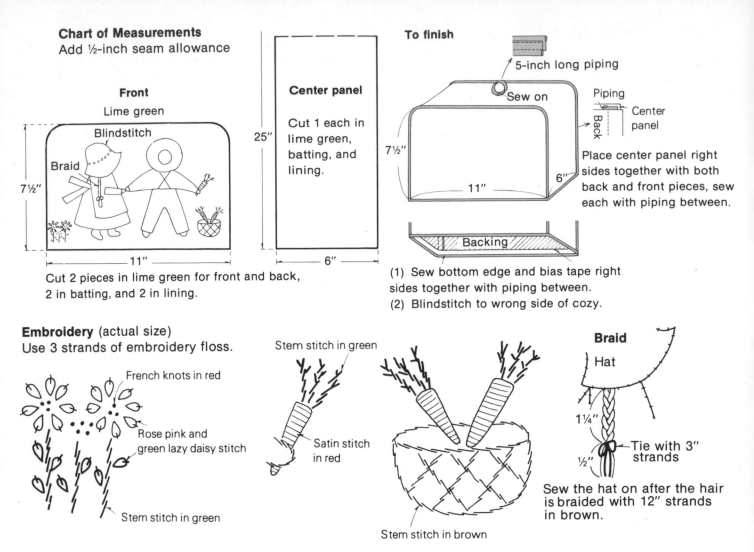

Chart of Measurements
Add ½-inch seam allowance

Front
Lime green

Blindstitch

Braid

7½"

11"

Cut 2 pieces in lime green for front and back,
2 in batting, and 2 in lining.

Center panel

Cut 1 each in
lime green,
batting, and
lining.

25"

6"

To finish

5-inch long piping

Sew on

Piping

Back

Center
panel

7½"

11"

6"

Place center panel right
sides together with both
back and front pieces, sew
each with piping between.

Backing

(1) Sew bottom edge and bias tape right
sides together with piping between.
(2) Blindstitch to wrong side of cozy.

Embroidery (actual size)
Use 3 strands of embroidery floss.

French knots in red

Rose pink and
green lazy daisy stitch

Stem stitch in green

Stem stitch in green

Satin stitch
in red

Stem stitch in brown

Braid

Hat

1¼"

½"

Tie with 3"
strands

Sew the hat on after the hair
is braided with 12" strands
in brown.

Tea Cozy
To make up:
(1) Scale up design (see page 36). Cut out pieces, adding ¼-inch
seam allowance.
(2) Cut front and back from lime green, as shown, adding ½-inch
seam allowance. Appliqué figures to front, using blindstitch, stuff
gently with filler. Embroider as indicated.
(3) Seam two pieces of red balloon right sides together, leave
opening to turn and stuff. Pin or baste batting on wrong side of
back and front pieces. Lay the two pieces right sides together,
catching balloon at top, as shown on page 85, and seam around
all but the straight bottom edge.
(4) Make up lining like outside. Turn up ½ inch on bottom edges
of outside and lining and blindstitch them together.

Patterns (actual size)
Add ¼-inch seam allowance

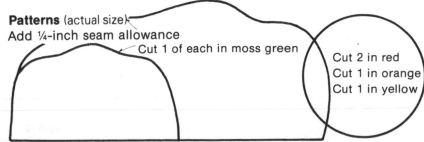

Cut 1 of each in moss green

Cut 2 in red
Cut 1 in orange
Cut 1 in yellow

Chart of Measurements

Front
Cut, adding ½-inch
seam allowance.

Red

Orange

Yellow

Blindstitch
and stuff

Stem stitch
in white

9½"

French knot in 6 strands of red

13"

Cut 2 pieces of lime green for front and back,
2 in batting, and 2 in lining.

To finish

Make balloon by seaming together two pieces of red, and filler.

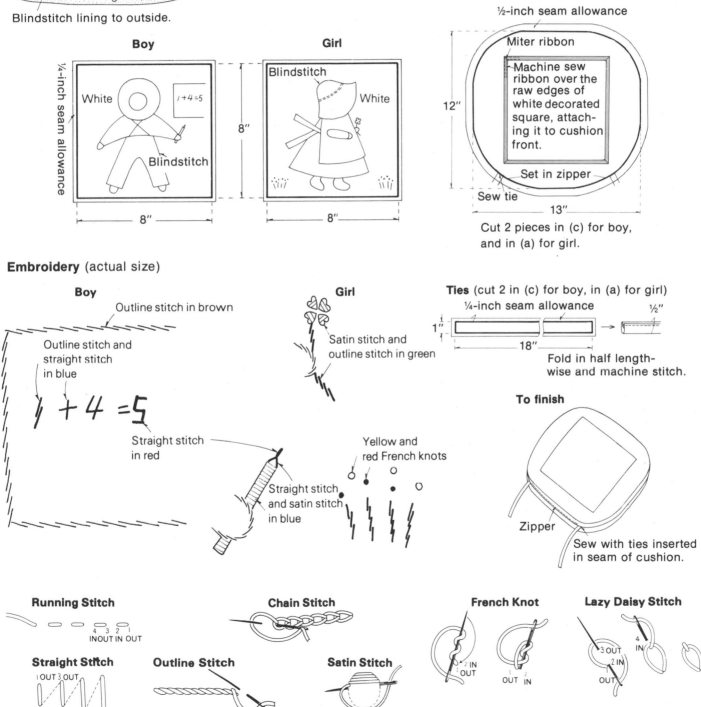

Blindstitch lining to outside.

Cushion

To make up:

(1) Enlarge and cut out appliqué pieces as for tea cozy and toaster cover.
(2) Appliqué designs with blindstitch to the 8-inch squares of white fabric. Finish with embroidery, as indicated.
(3) Cut out two pieces of print for cushion. Place the white square in the center of one and sew on with ribbon trim.
(4) Make up ties and sew them between back and front pieces, when seaming them right sides together, as shown on the chart.
(5) Sew zipper in place, as shown on the chart.

Chart of Measurements

½-inch seam allowance

Miter ribbon

Machine sew ribbon over the raw edges of white decorated square, attaching it to cushion front.

12"

Set in zipper

Sew tie

13"

Cut 2 pieces in (c) for boy, and in (a) for girl.

Boy

¼-inch seam allowance

White

$1 + 4 = 5$

Blindstitch

8"

8"

Girl

Blindstitch

White

8"

8"

Embroidery (actual size)

Boy

Outline stitch in brown

Outline stitch and straight stitch in blue

$1 + 4 = 5$

Straight stitch in red

Girl

Satin stitch and outline stitch in green

Straight stitch and satin stitch in blue

Yellow and red French knots

Ties (cut 2 in (c) for boy, in (a) for girl)

¼-inch seam allowance

1"

18"

½"

Fold in half lengthwise and machine stitch.

To finish

Zipper

Sew with ties inserted in seam of cushion.

Running Stitch

4 3 2 1
IN OUT IN OUT

Chain Stitch

French Knot

2 IN OUT

OUT IN

Lazy Daisy Stitch

3 OUT

4 IN

2 IN OUT

Straight Stitch

1 OUT 3 OUT

2 IN 4 IN

Outline Stitch

Satin Stitch

CUSHION
As shown on page 39

To make up:
(1) Cut patch pieces, adding ¼-inch seam allowance. Join as shown on page 38 and the chart.
(2) Place batting between pieced top and backing.
(3) Quilt as indicated.
(4) Cut out back pieces. Set in zipper. Seam front and back right sides together. Insert inner cushion.

Chart of Measurements

Front

Quilt on dotted line

16⅜"

16⅜"

Cut 1 piece in black 17 inches square for backing

Back   Add ½-inch seam allowance

Black-and-white polka dot print

Zipper opening

Add ½-inch seam allowance

16⅜"

12"

4⅜"

PATCHWORK PICTURE AND CUSHION
As shown on page 41

Patchwork Picture
To make up:
(1) Cut out patch pieces, adding ¼-inch seam allowance. Join as shown on page 40 and the chart.
(2) Lay batting between pieced top and backing. Quilt as indicated.

Chart of Measurements

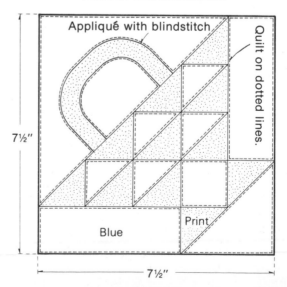

Appliqué with blindstitch

Quilt on dotted lines.

7½"

Blue

Print

7½"

Cushion

To make up:

(1) Assemble the pieces in the same general way shown on page 40, following the chart.

(2) Cut out back and front cushion pieces in (a). Appliqué pieced basket to center of front piece, as shown on the chart.

(3) Cut ties in (a). Sew them together

(4) Place ties as shown on the chart, catching them in the seam as you join the cushion back and front. Sew zipper in place.

To finish:

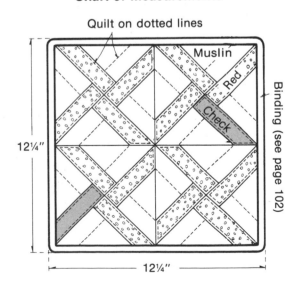

Sew, positioning ties as shown

Set in zipper

Chart of Measurements

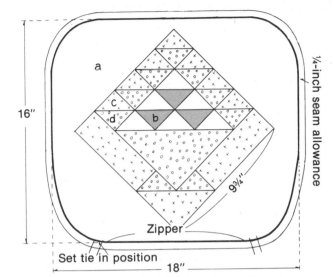

a

16"

c

d

b

9¾"

Zipper

¼-inch seam allowance

Set tie in position

18"

Cut front and back in (a), 16 inches × 18 inches, and round off corners.

Tie (cut 4)
¼-inch seam allowance

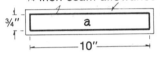

¾"

a

10"

⅜"

Fold in half lengthwise, turn in cut edge, machine stitch.

TABLE MAT AND TRAY CLOTH

As shown on page 47

Chart of Measurements

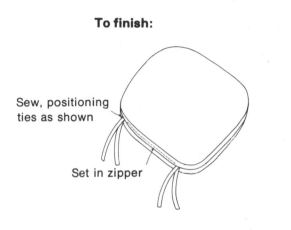

Quilt on dotted lines

Muslin

Red

Check

12¼"

12¼"

Binding (see page 102)

Tray cloth

To make up:

(1) Cut out patch pieces, adding ¼-inch seam allowance. Join as shown on page 46 and the chart.

(2) Lay batting between pieced top and backing. Quilt as indicated. Finish edges with binding.

Bias strip for binding
Moss green

¼-inch seam allowance

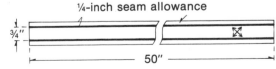

¾"

50"

87

Table Mat
To make up:
Work in the same way as for tray cloth.

Chart of Measurements

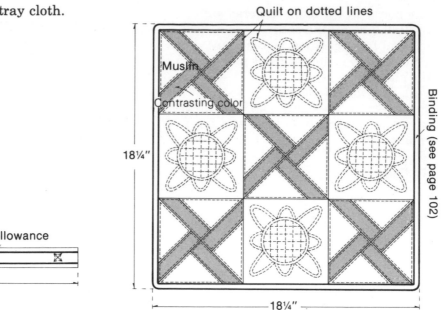

Quilt on dotted lines

Muslin

Contrasting color

18¼"

Binding (see page 102)

18¼"

Bias strip for binding

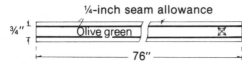

¼-inch seam allowance

¾"

Olive green

76"

MAT AND SMALL PURSE

As shown on page 53

Chart of Measurements

Mat
To make up:
(1) Cut out patch pieces, adding ¼-inch seam allowance. Join as shown on page 52 and the chart.
(2) Assemble pieced blocks with B blocks, as shown on the chart. Join borders to center, crosswise, then lengthwise.
(3) Lay batting between pieced top and backing.
(4) Quilt as indicated and finish the edges with binding.

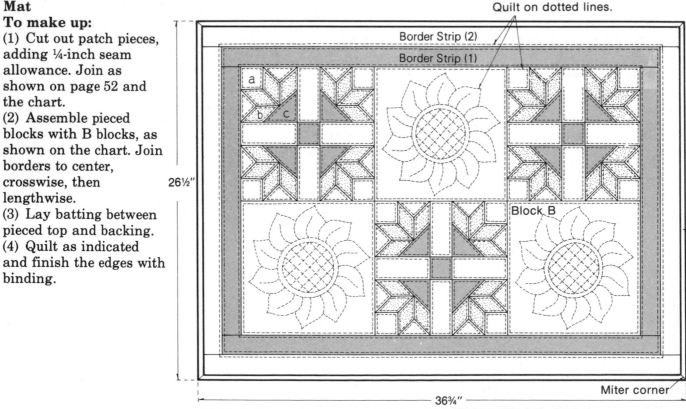

Quilt on dotted lines.

Border Strip (2)

Border Strip (1)

a

b c

26½"

Block B

Binding (see page 102)

Miter corner

36¾"

Cut block B from fabric (a), 10¼ inches square, plus seam allowance.
Cut backing from gold to a make piece 37¼ inches × 27 inches.

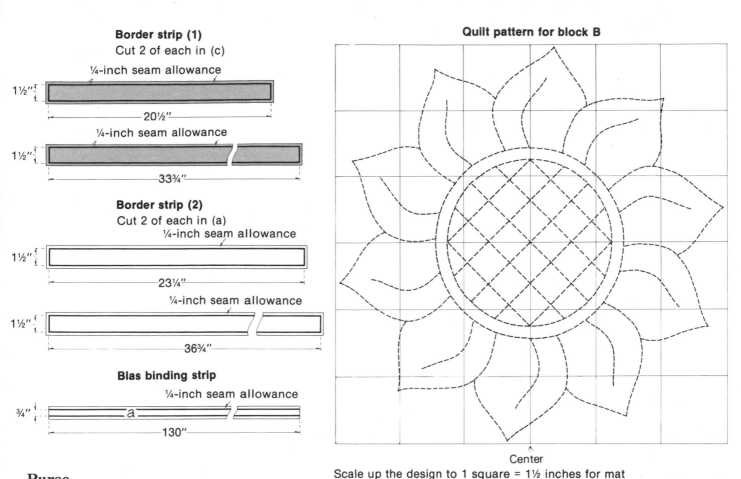

Border strip (1)
Cut 2 of each in (c)
¼-inch seam allowance

1½"
20½"

¼-inch seam allowance
1½"
33¾"

Border strip (2)
Cut 2 of each in (a)
¼-inch seam allowance

1½"
23¼"

¼-inch seam allowance
1½"
36¾"

Bias binding strip
¼-inch seam allowance
¾" a
130"

Quilt pattern for block B

Center

Scale up the design to 1 square = 1½ inches for mat
1 square = 1¼ inches for purse

Purse
To make up:
(1) Assemble patches as for the mat. Cut purse back piece from (a).
(2) Place batting and backing on wrong side of purse front and back, respectively.
(3) Quilt as indicated. Bind upper edge of each piece.

(4) Place front and back pieces together and stitch around 3 sides close to raw edge.
(5) Finish by binding the three edges and attaching shoulder strap, as shown on page 90.

Chart of Measurements

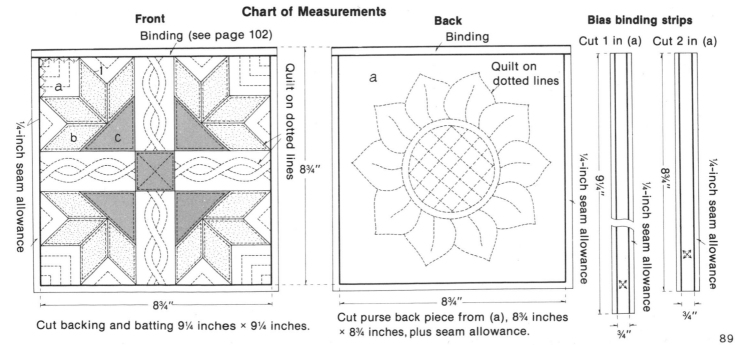

Front
Binding (see page 102)

¼-inch seam allowance

a

b c

Quilt on dotted lines

8¾"

8¾"

Cut backing and batting 9¼ inches × 9¼ inches.

Back
Binding

a

Quilt on dotted lines

¼-inch seam allowance

8¾"

Cut purse back piece from (a), 8¾ inches × 8¾ inches, plus seam allowance.

Bias binding strips
Cut 1 in (a)   Cut 2 in (a)

9¼"

¼-inch seam allowance

8¾"

¼-inch seam allowance

¾"   ¾"

89

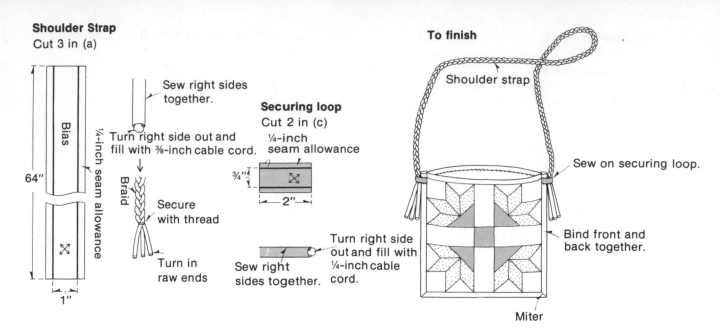

Shoulder Strap
Cut 3 in (a)

Bias

64"

¼-inch seam allowance

1"

Sew right sides together.

Turn right side out and fill with ⅜-inch cable cord.

Braid

Secure with thread

Turn in raw ends

Securing loop
Cut 2 in (c)

¼-inch seam allowance

¾"

2"

Turn right side out and fill with ¼-inch cable cord.

Sew right sides together.

To finish

Shoulder strap

Sew on securing loop.

Bind front and back together.

Miter

EYEGLASS CASES

As shown on page 49

To make up the navy-and-red case:
(1) Cut out patch pieces, adding ¼-inch seam allowance. Join as shown on page 48 and the chart.
(2) Cut 7-inch square, plus seam allowance, from navy print.
(3) Appliqué pieced motif, as shown, to square of fabric. Lay batting between decorated top and backing.
(4) Quilt as indicated.
(5) With right sides together, seam down center back. Finish seam with stitching or by turning in edge of backing over trimmed seam.
(6) Fold so that seam is in center back. Bind bottom edge together. Bind around open top edge.

Chart of Measurements

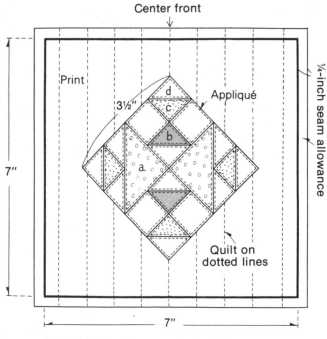

Center front

Print

d
c
3½"

Appliqué

b

a

7"

7"

¼-inch seam allowance

Quilt on dotted lines

Cut 7½-inch red square for backing.

Yardages and Number of Pieces	
Navy print	¼ yard
a (2 in #1)	scrap
b (2 in #2)	scrap
c (4 in #2)	scrap
d (10 in #2) (4 in #3)	scrap
Red	¼ yard

To finish

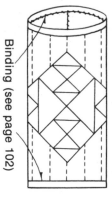

Binding (see page 102)

Binding strips

Cut 1 each in red
Add ¼-inch seam allowance

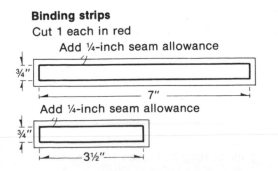

¾"

7"

Add ¼-inch seam allowance

¾"

3½"

To make up the green-and-purple case:
(1) Join the pieced blocks, as shown on page 48. Cut 2 green blocks to match, 3½ inches square plus seam allowance.
(2) Alternate the pieced and the green blocks and join, as shown on the chart. Lay the batting between the pieced top and the backing.
(3) Quilt as indicated.
(4) Repeat step (5) of navy-and-red case.
(5) Seam lower edge, bind around upper edge.

Chart of Measurements

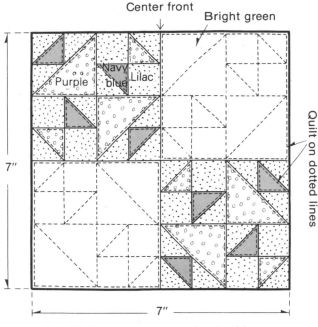

Center front
Bright green
Navy blue
Purple
Lilac

7"

Quilt on dotted lines

7"

Cut 7½-inch green square for backing.

To finish

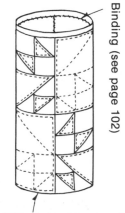

Binding (see page 102)

With right sides together, seam bottom edge.

Yardages and Number of Pieces	
Bright green	¼ yard
Purple (4 in #1) (4 in #2)	⅛ yard
Navy (8 in #2)	scrap
Lilac (20 in #2) (8 in #3)	⅛ yard

Binding strip
Cut 1 in bright green

¼-inch seam allowance

¾"

7"

RUNNER AND PLACEMATS

As shown on page 55

Placemat
To make up:
(1) Cut out patch pieces and join as shown on page 54 and the chart.
(2) With right sides together, seam border strips to ends. Press, and lay batting on wrong side. Quilt along the the seamlines.
(3) Fold and mark the center at ends of both pieced top and lining. With right sides facing, seam lining to top along ends.
(4) Turn piece right side out, bring lining over long edges, turn under ¼-inch seam allowance, and baste in place to form side borders. Blind-stitch with matching thread. Topstitch all around border.

Chart of Measurements

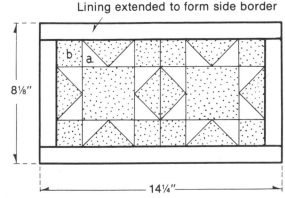

Lining extended to form side border

8⅛"

b a

14¼"

End border strips
Cut 2 in (a)

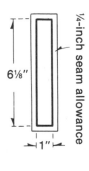

6⅛"

¼-inch seam allowance

1"

Cut lining in fabric (a), 14¼ inches × 10⅛ inches, plus ¼-inch seam allowance.
Cut batting 14¼ inches × 8⅛ inches.

Table Runner
To make up:
Work in the same way as for the placemat (page 91).

Chart of Measurements

Lining extended to form side border

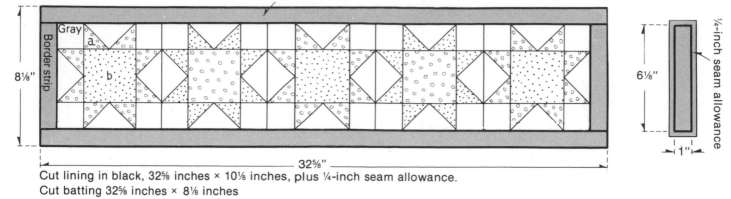

Gray
a
b
Border strip

8⅛″

32⅝″

Cut lining in black, 32⅝ inches × 10⅛ inches, plus ¼-inch seam allowance.
Cut batting 32⅝ inches × 8⅛ inches

End border strips
Cut 2 in black

¼-inch seam allowance

6⅛″

1″

POTHOLDER AND TABLE RUNNER
As shown on page 57

Table Runner
To make up:
(1) Join pieces as shown on page 56.
(2) Work as for placemat (page 91), adding sash strips between blocks.

Chart of Measurements

Lining extended to form side border

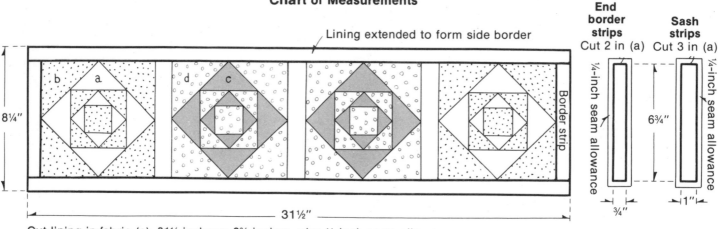

b   a   d   c   Border strip

8¼″

31½″

Cut lining in fabric (a), 31½ inches × 9¾ inches, plus ¼-inch seam allowance.
Cut batting 31½ inches × 8¼ inches

End border strips
Cut 2 in (a)   **Sash strips**
Cut 3 in (a)

¼-inch seam allowance   ¼-inch seam allowance

6¾″

¾″   1″

Potholder
To make up:
(1) Join pieces as shown on page 56.
(2) Work as for placemat—but use two layers of batting and quilt after the lining is in place (by machine if preferred).

Chart of Measurements

Lining extended to form side border

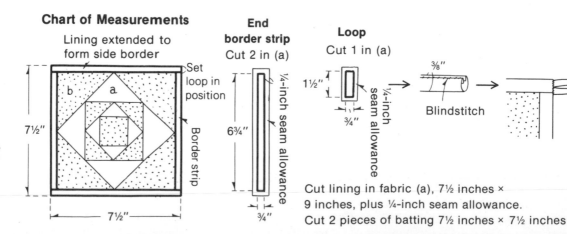

b   a   Set loop in position   Border strip

7½″

7½″

End border strip
Cut 2 in (a)

¼-inch seam allowance

6¾″

¾″

Loop
Cut 1 in (a)

1½″

¾″   ¼-inch seam allowance

⅜″

Blindstitch

Cut lining in fabric (a), 7½ inches × 9 inches, plus ¼-inch seam allowance.
Cut 2 pieces of batting 7½ inches × 7½ inches

CRIB QUILT
As shown on page 43

Muslin

Rust

67"

Border strip

Binding (see page 102)

Quilt on dotted lines.

44½"

Cut backing in pale pink and batting 67½ inches × 45 inches

To make up:
(1) Cut out patch pieces, adding ¼-inch seam allowance. Join as shown on page 42 and the chart.
(2) Lay batting between pieced top and backing.
(3) Quilt as indicated. Bind edges lengthwise, then crosswise.

Yellow
= a b
Cut 9 (a–b)

Yellow
= c d
Cut 7 (c–d)

Yellow
= c e
Cut 27 (c–e)

Lime green
= a e
Cut 21 (a–e)

Yellow
= a f
Cut 15 (a–f)

Yellow
= g h
Cut 9 (g–h)

Gold
= c d
Cut 3 (c–d)

Border strips
Cut 2 of each in pale pink
¼-inch seam allowance
2"
44½"
¼-inch seam allowance
2"
63"

Binding strips Cut 2 of each in rust
¼-inch seam allowance
1½"
44½"
¼-inch seam allowance
1½"
66½"

To finish binding

Blindstitch
Wrong side

93

WALL HANGING AND BAGS

As shown on page 59

Wall Hanging
To make up:
(1) Cut out patch pieces, adding ¼-inch seam allowance. Join as shown on page 58 and the chart.
(2) Lay batting between pieced top and lining. Turn under raw edge ¼ inch and bring lining over the edge to form ¼-inch border. Blindstitch it in place.
(3) Quilt along seamlines.
(4) Sew loop and button in place on back of each block.

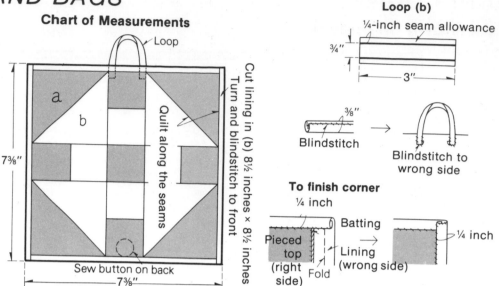

Chart of Measurements

Loop

a

b

Quilt along the seams

7⅜"

Sew button on back

7⅜"

Cut lining in (b) 8½ inches × 8½ inches
Turn and blindstitch to front

Loop (b)

¼-inch seam allowance

¾"

3"

⅜"

Blindstitch

Blindstitch to wrong side

To finish corner

¼ inch

Pieced top (right side)

Batting

Lining (wrong side)

Fold

¼ inch

Bags
To make up:
(1) Assemble patches as for wall hanging. Lay batting between pieced block and backing, quilt along seams.
(2) Cut out bag pieces in (e), as shown on the chart. Turn under edges of pieced block ¼ inch, baste in position to bag front, and topstitch in place.

(3) Make up strap by folding and topstitching edges. Seam ends of yoke piece, sides and bottom of bag pieces. Lay handles to bottom edge of yoke, as shown, seam to bag, and topstitch for added strength.
(4) Miter lower corners to make a 2-inch base. Seam lining together and drop into bag. Blindstitch turned top edge of lining to turned top edge of bag.

Chart of Measurements

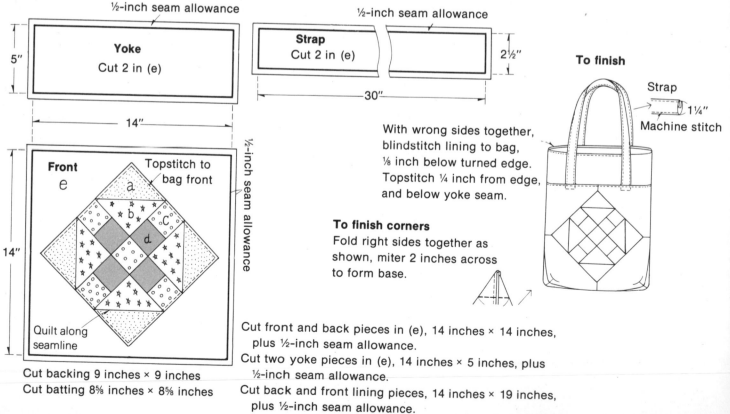

½-inch seam allowance

Yoke Cut 2 in (e)

5"

14"

½-inch seam allowance

Front e

a

b c

d

14"

Quilt along seamline

Topstitch to bag front

½-inch seam allowance

½-inch seam allowance

Strap Cut 2 in (e)

2½"

30"

With wrong sides together, blindstitch lining to bag, ⅛ inch below turned edge. Topstitch ¼ inch from edge, and below yoke seam.

To finish corners
Fold right sides together as shown, miter 2 inches across to form base.

To finish

Strap

Machine stitch

1¼"

Cut backing 9 inches × 9 inches
Cut batting 8⅝ inches × 8⅝ inches

Cut front and back pieces in (e), 14 inches × 14 inches, plus ½-inch seam allowance.
Cut two yoke pieces in (e), 14 inches × 5 inches, plus ½-inch seam allowance.
Cut back and front lining pieces, 14 inches × 19 inches, plus ½-inch seam allowance.

QUILT AND SEWING POCKET
As shown on page 51

To make up:

(1) Cut out patch pieces, adding ¼-inch seam allowance. Join as shown on page 50 and block A chart.

(2) Cut out 24 blue blocks for A and B. Appliqué pieced motifs on 12 of them with a blindstitch.

(3) Working in rows across the quilt, seam A and B alternately, as shown on the chart, with sash C betweeen.

(4) Seam sashes C to corner blocks D, as shown on the chart.

(5) Join block strips with sash strips for length of quilt, as shown in the chart.

(6) Lay batting between finished top and backing. Quilt as indicated in B blocks, also around motifs and around all blocks.

(7) Seam border strips together to make a frame. With right side of border to wrong side of quilt, pin and seam all around.

(8) Turn under inner edge of border ¼-inch and topstitch both edges in place with quilting stitch.

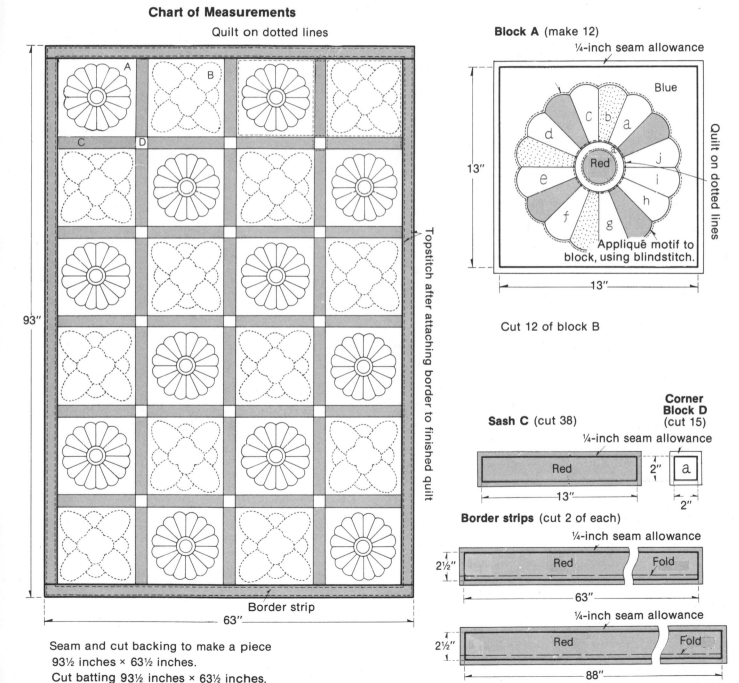

Chart of Measurements

Quilt on dotted lines

Topstitch after attaching border to finished quilt

93″

63″

Border strip

Seam and cut backing to make a piece 93½ inches × 63½ inches.

Cut batting 93½ inches × 63½ inches.

Block A (make 12)

¼-inch seam allowance

Blue

Quilt on dotted lines

Red

Appliqué motif to block, using blindstitch.

13″

13″

Cut 12 of block B

Sash C (cut 38)

Red

13″

2″

Corner Block D (cut 15)

¼-inch seam allowance

a

2″

2″

Border strips (cut 2 of each)

¼-inch seam allowance

Red

Fold

2½″

63″

¼-inch seam allowance

Red

Fold

2½″

88″

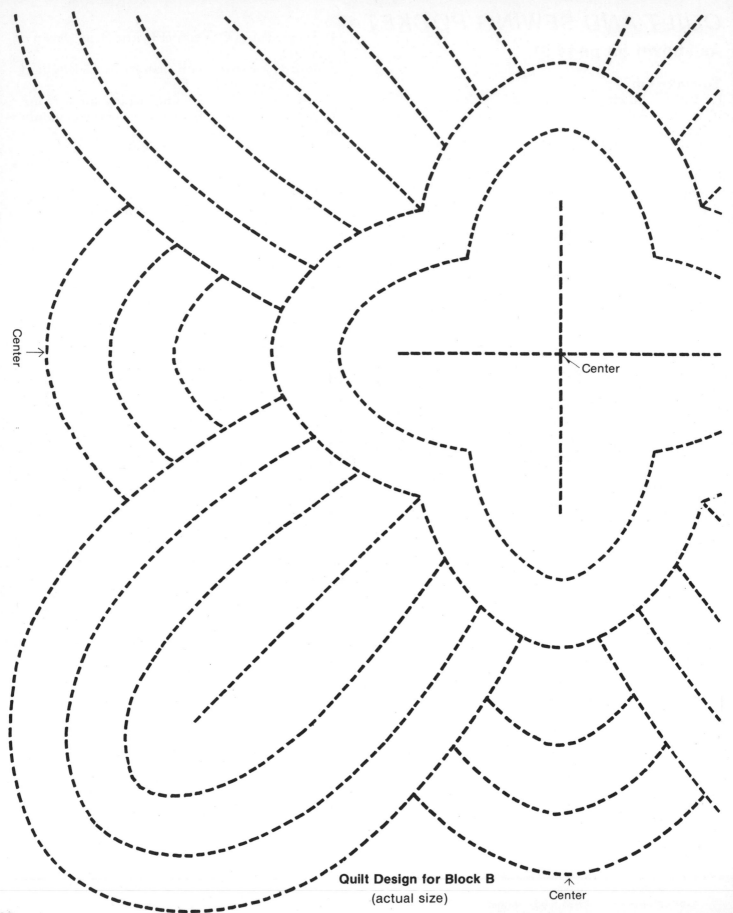

Center

Center

Quilt Design for Block B
(actual size)

Center

Sewing Pocket
To make up:
(1) Assemble the motif as for the quilt.
(2) Cut front and back, as shown, round off lower corners. Appliqué the motif to the front, using a blindstitch.

(3) Place batting and backing on wrong side of front and back pieces and quilt, as indicated. Bind top edges.
(4) Lay the two quilted pieces back to back and stitch close to raw edge. Bind around, making strap and loop, as shown.

Chart of Measurements

Front
Binding (see page 102)

Appliqué motif to block, using blindstitch.

c
d
e
f
a
b
a

¼-inch seam allowance

Quilt on dotted lines.

6½"

7"

Cut backing in fabric (b) and batting same size as top piece.

Back
Binding (see page 102)

a

¼-inch seam allowance

Quilt on dotted lines.

6½"

Bias strip for strap and binding

a

60"

¼-inch seam allowance

¾"

Bias binding strip (cut 2)

¼-inch seam allowance

¾"

a

7"

To finish

Strap continued from binding

Loop

Extend binding 2 inches to form loop. Sew to back.

Bind with front and back wrong sides together.

PEN CASE AND PHONE SET
As shown on page 61

Phone Set
To make up the phone cover:
(1) Cut out patch pieces, adding ¼-inch seam allowance. Join as shown on page 60 and the chart.
(2) Place pieced top and lining wrong sides together, turn edges of lining over top piece, miter corners with a blindstitch, turn ¼-inch under along edge, and topstitch in place.

To make up the mat:
(1) Assemble patches as for phone cover.
(2) Lay batting between pieced top and backing. Quilt as indicated.
(3) Bind edges to finish.

Chart of Measurements

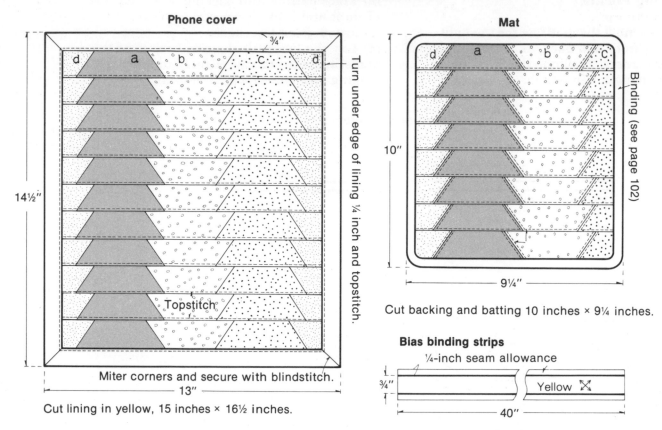

Phone cover

d a b c d

¾″

Turn under edge of lining ¼ inch and topstitch.

14½″

Topstitch

Miter corners and secure with blindstitch.

13″

Cut lining in yellow, 15 inches × 16½ inches.

Mat

d a b c

10″

Binding (see page 102)

9¼″

Cut backing and batting 10 inches × 9¼ inches.

Bias binding strips

¼-inch seam allowance

¾″

Yellow ⊠

40″

Pen Case

To make up:

(1) Assemble patches as for phone cover.

(2) On both pieces lay batting between pieced top and backing. Quilt as indicated.

(3) Bind upper front edge.

(4) Lay front and back wrong sides together, baste, and bind around, rounding corners slightly.

Chart of Measurements

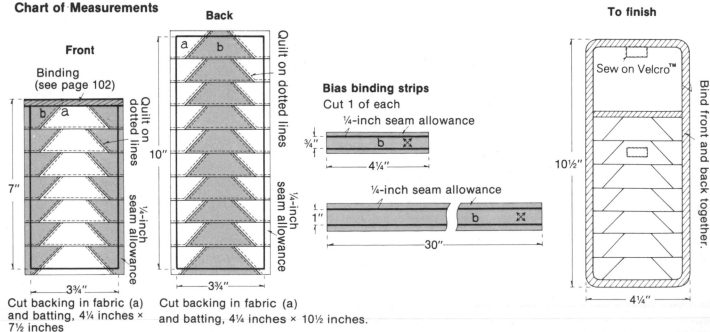

Front

Binding (see page 102)

b a

Quilt on dotted lines

7″

¼-inch seam allowance

3¾″

Cut backing in fabric (a) and batting, 4¼ inches × 7½ inches

Back

a b

Quilt on dotted lines

10″

¼-inch seam allowance

3¾″

Cut backing in fabric (a) and batting, 4¼ inches × 10½ inches.

Bias binding strips

Cut 1 of each

¼-inch seam allowance

¾″

b ⊠

4¼″

¼-inch seam allowance

1″

b ⊠

30″

To finish

Sew on Velcro™

10½″

Bind front and back together.

4¼″

CUSHION AND BAGS

As shown on page 63

Cushion
To make up:
(1) Cut out patch pieces, adding ¼-inch seam allowance. Join as shown on page 62 and the chart.

(2) Join the borders to the pieced front. Lay batting and backing on wrong side.
(3) Quilt as indicated.
(4) Cut out back pieces. Stitch zipper in place. Seam each edge of back to edge of border, mitering the corners of the borders as you go.

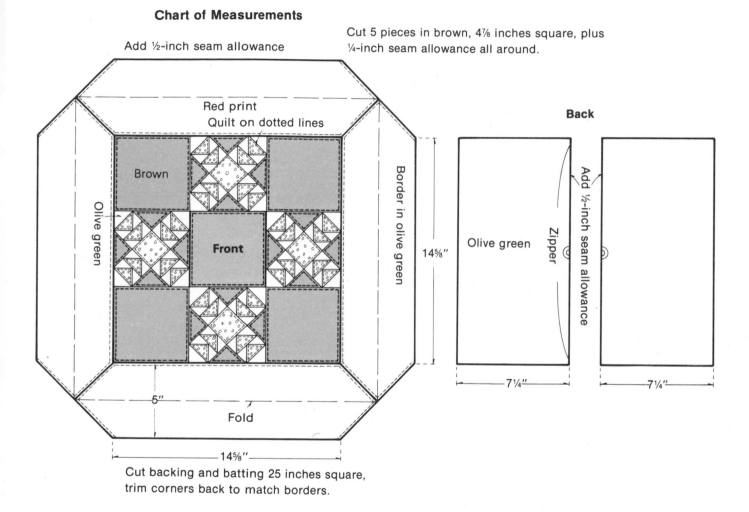

Chart of Measurements

Add ½-inch seam allowance

Cut 5 pieces in brown, 4⅞ inches square, plus ¼-inch seam allowance all around.

Red print
Quilt on dotted lines

Brown

Olive green

Front

Border in olive green

14⅝"

Back

Olive green

Zipper

Add ½-inch seam allowance

7¼"

7¼"

5"

Fold

14⅝"

Cut backing and batting 25 inches square, trim corners back to match borders.

Bags
To make up navy bag (bottom right):
(1) Cut and assemble patches as shown on page 62, making two blocks. Join, as shown in the chart on page 100, with 3 white strips.
(2) Lay batting and backing on wrong side of pieced strip. Quilt as indicated.
(3) Cut bag back and front pieces. Turn under top and side edges of strip and topstitch in place on bag front.
(4) Make up handle and lining.
(5) Drop lining into bag, wrong sides together. Turn top of both to make hem and machine stitch in place. Machine stitch handles to top of bag.

To make up white bag (top right)
(1) Join patches for pocket, as shown on page 62. Cut pocket lining. Lay the two right sides together and seam around, leaving opening for turning. Turn and topstitch, as shown on page 100.
(2) Lay batting on wrong side of bag pieces. Quilt as indicated. Lay pocket in position on front and topstitch in place.
(3) Finish bag as for navy bag, above.

Navy Bag
(bottom right)

Chart of Measurements

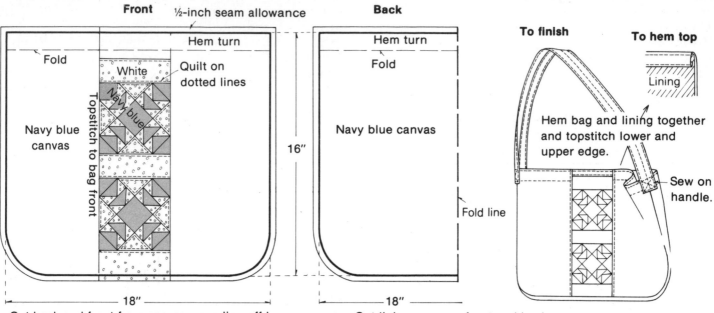

Front

½-inch seam allowance

Hem turn

Fold

White

Quilt on dotted lines

Navy blue

Topstitch to bag front

Navy blue canvas

Back

Hem turn

Fold

Navy blue canvas

16"

Fold line

To finish

Hem bag and lining together and topstitch lower and upper edge.

To hem top

Lining

Sew on handle.

18"

18"

Cut back and front from canvas, rounding off lower corners. Cut lining same as front and back.
Cut batting 4⅞ inches × 14¼ inches. Cut backing 5⅜ inches × 14¾ inches.

Handle
Cut 1 in navy blue canvas.

¼-inch seam allowance

3"

36"

Selvage

1½"

Machine stitch

White Bag
(top right)

To finish

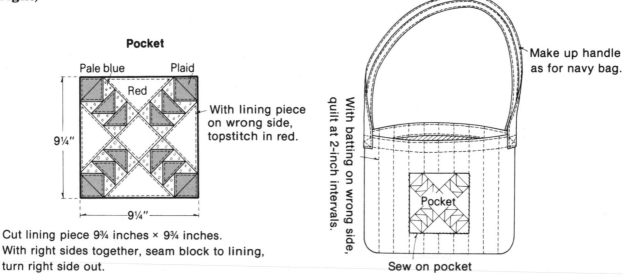

Pocket

Pale blue   Plaid

Red

9¼"

9¼"

With lining piece on wrong side, topstitch in red.

With batting on wrong side, quilt at 2-inch intervals.

Make up handle as for navy bag.

Pocket

Sew on pocket

Cut lining piece 9¾ inches × 9¾ inches.
With right sides together, seam block to lining, turn right side out.

Cut front and back from white canvas, same size as navy bag.
Cut batting and lining same size. Line as navy bag.

PATCHWORK TECHNIQUES

CUTTING
(1) Cut out the actual size pattern in firm cardboard.

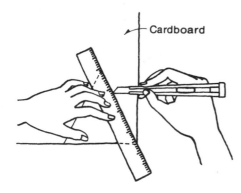

Cardboard

(2) Place the cardboard shape (called a template) on the fabric and draw around it accurately. Add a ¼-inch seam allowance before cutting out. (Accuracy is imperative if a good result is to be achieved.)

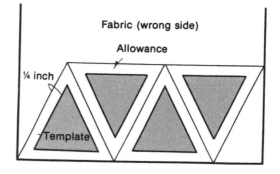

Fabric (wrong side)

Allowance

¼ inch

Template

JOINING
Using Paper Linings:
Although this traditional method takes time and effort, the result is impressive.

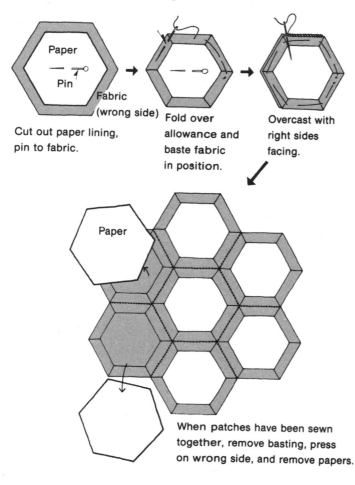

Paper

Pin

Fabric (wrong side)

Cut out paper lining, pin to fabric.

Fold over allowance and baste fabric in position.

Overcast with right sides facing.

Paper

Paper

When patches have been sewn together, remove basting, press on wrong side, and remove papers.

Joining Patches by Hand:
A common method of joining simple patches. Press seam allowance to one side (preferably toward darker color so that seams are less obvious).

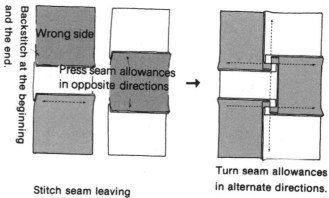

Backstitch at the beginning and the end.

Wrong side

Press seam allowances in opposite directions

Turn seam allowances in alternate directions. Press open corners.

Stitch seam leaving seam allowances free at each edge.

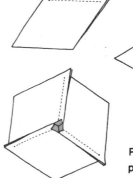

Press seams in same direction, press center flat.

Joining Patches by Machine:

A good way to make up large items. Seams are usually pressed open but sometimes turned to one side so a dark color does not show through a light one.

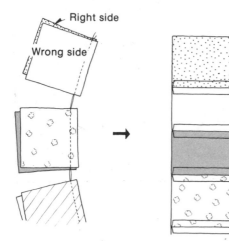

Right side

Wrong side

Stitch pieces together without cutting thread, then join pairs to make a row.

QUILTING

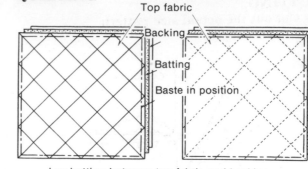

Top fabric

Backing

Batting

Baste in position

Lay batting between top fabric and backing, baste in position and quilt with machine or running stitch.

Angle of the Needle

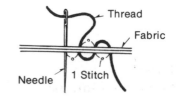

Thread

Fabric

Needle   1 Stitch

Insert needle at 90° to fabric.

BINDING

①

Stitch binding fabric

Right side of
top fabric

Position binding strip and stitch.

② **Machine sewing**

Binding fabric

Machine
stitch

Right side of
top fabric

Fold strip to wrong side. Stitch next to the binding from right side, catching under edge of binding.

Binding fabric

Wrong side

Hand sewing

Binding fabric

Wrong side

Fold the binding strip to wrong side, blindstitch.

BLINDSTITCH

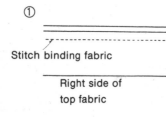

Turning

Make small stitches at right angles to the edge with matching thread.

MAKING BIAS STRIPS

Method (A)

Cutting

Joining

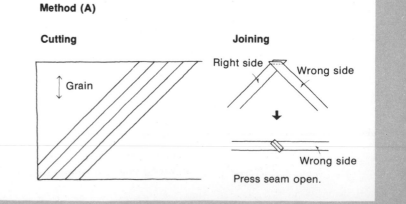

Grain

Right side

Wrong side

Wrong side

Press seam open.

Method (B)

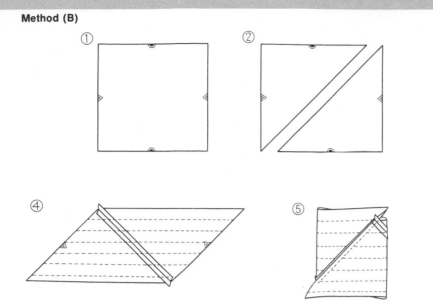

① ② ③

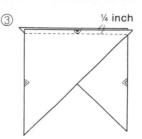

¼ inch

Sew right sides together,
matching marks (•) exactly.

④

Press seam open, mark lines at
intervals of the width required.

⑤

Match edges marked (•), right sides
together, and join, leaving one width
extending at each end.

⑥

Press seam open.
Cut along the line.

Suggested mail-order sources for quilting supplies:

Quilts & Other Comforts
Box 394
Wheatridge, Colorado 80033

Cabin Fever Calicoes
Box 6256
Washington, D.C. 20015

Ginger Snap Station
P.O. Box 81086
Atlanta, Georgia 30366

Mrs. Wigg's Cabbage Patch, Inc.
2600 Beaver Avenue
Des Moines, Iowa 50310

The Silver Thimble
249 High Street
Ipswich, Massachusetts 01938

The Quiltworks
218 3rd Avenue
Minneapolis, Minnesota 55401

Quilt Country
500 Nichols Road
Kansas City, Missouri 64112

Mail-in
P.O. Box 603
Woodcliff Lake, New Jersey 07675

Gutcheon Patchworks
611 Broadway
New York, New York 10012

Cross Patch
Rt. #9
Garrison, New York 10524

Creative Quilt Center
Stearns & Foster
Box 15380
Cincinnati, Ohio 45215

Contemporary Quilts
3466 Summer Avenue
Memphis, Tennessee 38122

Great Expectations
155 Town and County Village
Houston, Texas 77024

Let's Quilt and Sew-on
P.O. Box 29526
San Antonio, Texas 78229

Calico Country Store
10822 124th Street
Edmonton, Alberta
Canada   T5M 0H3